A Time to Die
A Handbook for Funeral Sermons

A · TIME · TO · DIE

A HANDBOOK FOR FUNERAL SERMONS

Includes Sample Sermons for Difficult Funerals

KENT D. RICHMOND

ABINGDON PRESS
Nashville

A TIME TO DIE:
A HANDBOOK FOR FUNERAL SERMONS

Copyright © 1990 by Abingdon Press

This book is printed on acid-free paper.

Library of Congress Cataloging-in-Publication Data

Richmond, Kent D., 1939-
    A time to die : a handbook for preparing funeral sermons / Kent D. Richmond.
        p. cm.
    Includes bibliographical references.
    ISBN 0-687-42122-5 (alk. paper)
    1. Funeral sermons. 2. Sermons, American. 3. Funeral sermons—History and criticism. 4. Death. 5. Funeral rites and ceremonies.
    I. Title.
BV4275.R53   1990
252'.1—dc20
                                     90-32934
                                         CIP

All Scripture quotations, unless otherwise noted, are from the Revised Standard Version of the Bible, copyrighted 1946, 1952, © 1971, 1973. Used by permission.

All Scripture quotations marked KJV are from the King James Version of the Bible.

MANUFACTURED IN THE UNITED STATES OF AMERICA

For My Parents,

Kenneth and Harriet Richmond

CONTENTS

PREFACE

Job placement interviews often are highly tense affairs in which the success of the applicant can hinge upon how well a single question is answered. Under the United Methodist appointive system, of which I am a part, the interview with a Pastor-Parish Relations Committee tends to be less highly charged. It is understood at the outset that, once the prospective pastor consents to an interview by the committee, he also has consented to the appointment. Only rarely does the interviewing committee find a reason to ask that the appointment not be made. Of the interviews that I have experienced, the one that I most remember is the interview in which one of the committee members asked me, "What are your strengths and weaknesses?"

The frankness of the question caught me offguard. I suspect that was what she intended. My answer returned the favor. I replied that I felt funerals and funeral preaching to be one of the most meaningful

areas of my ministry. As for the weaknesses, I will
beg the question. The reader will have ample
opportunity to determine whether the author's
estimate seems correct. My questioner chose not to
pursue the answer. The discomfort many of us feel
with the subject of death causes us to move quickly to
more congenial subjects.

This is a book that deals with death. More
specifically, it is a book that attempts to provide help
for those who must preach in the presence of death,
particularly those deaths that are among the most
difficult. There are many persons whose contribution has helped this book come to birth. Chief among
them are all of the bereaved families who admitted
me into their grief. A simple "thank you" does not
begin to help express the gratitude that I feel for all
that they taught me over almost thirty years of parish
ministry. It is through my journey with them that
this book began.

I would also express my appreciation and respect
to my colleagues in the Department of Pastoral Care
at Lutheran General Hospital in Park Ridge, Illinois.
The opening chapter of this book was presented to
them at one of our peer review sessions, and benefits
from their suggestions.

Appreciation must also go to the staff of the United
Library at Garrett-Evangelical and Seabury Western
Theological Seminaries for help provided in the
location of research materials, and to my pastor, the
Reverend John E. Sumwalt, for spur-of-the-moment
assistance in finding a reference in a volume that I
did not have in my possession.

Special appreciation must go to Donald F. Chatfield of Garrett-Evangelical Theological Seminary and Donald M. Wardlaw of McCormick Theological Seminary for help in identifying recent books in homiletics that may provide further reading for issues connected to the sermons that make up chapter 4 of this book.

Although the weaknesses remain those of the author, every book contains strengths that reflect the skill of those who do the editing. Thanks to Abingdon's Gregory Michael, who encouraged me to think about this book, and to Paul Franklyn, Sally Sharpe, and Don Baker, whose editorial skill made it easier to organize the material in a manner both flowing and concise.

Finally, much love to my family. My wife, Dorothy, listened to endless readings of chapter-sections, and helped with the typing. She is my definition of patience. My sons, Tim and Steve, relinquished me to a summer and fall spent behind a typewriter rather than a canoe paddle. Next year on the Pike, guys!

INTRODUCTION

Don't solve my problems by telling me death is a
good idea, death is a step up. And don't talk to me
about some philosophical distinction called my soul.
Talk about me. Because death is my enemy. Death
kills me.

ROBERT FARRAR CAPON[1]

Well, I know you're busy, so that's all for now. P. S. I
never believed any of those stories going around a
few years ago that 'God is dead.' How could you be?
We don't have one weapon that can shoot that far.

MIKE ROYKO[2]

"Where does it hurt?" the doctor asked. He
watched carefully as my son pointed to the injury.
"Does it hurt here?" he asked. "What about here?"
Little by little, by palpating around the injury, he was
able to isolate the area of pain, understand what

had happened to my son, and arrange treatment
that, in time, took away the hurt.

"Isn't it wonderful what medical science can do
these days!" is an often-heard comment. But some of
the physicians with whom I work would be the first to
balance that comment with the recognition that
there is also much that medical science cannot do.
Although my son's fractured arm was simply treated
and the pain was quickly removed, there are other
hurts less easily healed. There is a pain that arises
deep within all of us which medication can only ease,
not remove. When death takes someone we deeply
love, it occasions an anguish at the very center of our
being, an anguish that may threaten to tear our lives
asunder. Time and again, while employed as a
hospital chaplain, I've sat with families at the
moment in which their physician has brought them
word of the death of their loved one. As much as is
possible for an outsider, I have felt the wrench in my
own being, not only because of the death that has
taken place, but also because I know that at the
moment the physician is saying, "I'm sorry" to the
family, he is also saying, "O.K., pastor, now it's your
turn."

Death is a boundary event; it waits for us at the
edge, the boundary of our lives. Its pain demands the
presence of a person whose calling moves him to
walk the boundaries with the bereaved and to bring
to death's challenge a word of hope.

If our speech seems at first tentative, it is only
because we are so profoundly aware of what we are
about. Ernest Becker says that "man's terror is

always 'holy terror'—which is a strikingly apt popular phrase. Terror always refers to the ultimates of life and death."[3] Something very similar can be said of our speech at the moment of dying. It is holy speech, speech that reflects awareness of death's threat to all that we hold sacred and yet states "Even so, believe!"

This is a book for the pastor who would speak that word of faith. It comes from a working pastor who, through many years in the parish ministry and now as a chaplain at a major metropolitan hospital and trauma center, has walked and continues to walk with families on the boundary of death. More particularly, it is the book of a pastor whose training focuses in the areas of homiletics and pastoral care. It is written in the hope that insights from this involvement will bring help to other pastors in their ministry to those who grieve.

The book has two focuses. The first of these is that of understanding what is happening to those who confront death and pass through the dynamics of grief that it arouses. The second is related to, and in some sense springs from, the first. To put it very simply: How do we preach to those who grieve, particularly under very difficult circumstances such as the death of a child, or a suicide?

The first chapter examines death's effect upon us, especially its threat to meaning. Chapter 2 looks at the context in which we bring our word of hope to bear upon death's assault on meaning: the funeral or memorial service. Chapter 3 walks through the process of sermon preparation and lifts up the message that we bring. The fourth chapter examines resources and provides sample sermons that have been meaningful to families who have gone through some of the most difficult deaths that any of us will ever encounter.

Edgar Jackson has described our culture as "death-denying and death-defying," a culture that "tends to isolate and leave the grief-stricken emotionally unsupported."[4] It is my hope that this volume will help the pastor provide support for persons facing the boundary between death's anguish and life's dawning joy.

Notes

1. *Exit 36* (New York: Seabury Press, 1975), pp. 25-26.
2. The *Chicago Sun-Times,* May 5, 1981.
3. *The Denial of Death* (New York: The Free Press, 1973), p. 150.
4. "Why You Should Understand Grief: A Minister's View," in *But Not to Lose: A Book of Comfort for Those Bereaved,* ed. Austin H. Kutscher (New York: Frederick Fell, 1969), p. 46.

CHAPTER ONE

Death's Threat to Meaning

These days . . . one has the impression, at least in
America, that death has been all too much found.
Much more elusive is the psychological relationship
between the phenomenon of death and the flow of
life.

ROBERT JAY LIFTON[1]

That it's rough out there and chancy is no surprise.
Every live thing is a survivor on a kind of extended
emergency bivouac.

ANNIE DILLARD[2]

"It stinks; it really does," she said. That was
Pam's reaction to being told by her physician that her
cancer had spread. A divorced mother of five children,
she had struggled to hold her family together through
all of the pain of her divorce, the subsequent financial
strain, and the discipline problems that emerged in her
children. That she had managed it successfully only
made the metastatic diagnosis appear even more
unjust. To have managed to sustain her and her
family's lives only to find herself confronting the
possibility of her own death made the situation

17

almost more than she could bear. "Why me?" she asked. "What did I do to deserve this?"

Pam's question illustrates the impact death has on us through its challenge to our sense of specialness.[3] Through our childhood years, we are protected by our parents and nurtured on a diet of rhymes and stories in which happy endings seem to be the rule. There are many in our society who still hold to a puritan tendency to view personal success as a mark of God's favor. There is a popular form of American "religion" that makes the Golden Rule its focus; its adherents can be found in our congregations. These people feel that, if they deal gently with others, God should return the favor. Whatever the cause, many of us grow into adulthood with a strong sense that God owes us "special" protection from life's pain.

Parts of the New Testament feed this sense of personal invulnerability. It tells us that we have been created only a little lower than the angels (Heb. 2:7, 9), that the very hairs of our heads are numbered by the God who loves us intimately (Matt. 10:30). We are urged to ask for whatever we need in the faith that God will grant it (Matt. 21:22). It is a rude awakening to discover that we are not as invulnerable as we thought. Tolstoy's Ivan Ilyich expressed our sense of disbelief that "for me . . . Ivan Ilyich, with all my thoughts and emotions, it's altogether a different matter. It cannot be that I ought to die. That would be too terrible."[4] When it becomes obvious that death is not only something that happens to other people, that death will bring an end to *my* life, it raises a crisis of meaning. Death's greatest threat is that of separation from all that holds meaning for us. We experience this in three areas of our lives: ourselves, our relationships, and our faith.

Death threatens to separate me, first, from my own life and its accomplishments. Jesus' story of the wealthy farmer (Luke 12:16-21) reminds us of the tenuous nature of our accomplishments, but we build our bigger barns nonetheless. We come to enjoy the sense of respect accorded us by others. The little perks and privileges that denote prominence in our society bolster our sense of self-esteem and self-importance, as indeed they should. But when we allow our accomplishments to make us feel that there is no end to what we can accomplish, death's corrective comes like a splash of cold water in the heat of our enthusiasm. Whereas we have extended our reach into interstellar space, there is yet

> one glaring exception to this paean of man's conquests, one problem where all of his assurance, ingenuity, and wit avail him nothing; an area which stands in bold contrast to the rest of nature which is so malleable to his will . . . the phenomenon of death. Here man, with all his cleverness, is powerless. He may postpone death, he may assuage its physical pains, he may rationalize it away or deny its very existence, but escape it he cannot.[5]

If we link a sense of immortality to our accomplishments, particularly when middle-age first forces us to confront the question of how we will be remembered, then death reminds us that "this night your soul is required of you; and the things you have prepared, whose will they be?" (Luke 12:20).

Death threatens us, second, with separation from the persons we love. This is the fear most often voiced by persons who talk with me about dying. We are social beings; we live in relationship, and it is from our relationships that we receive our greatest sense of being loved and valued. I may receive some small amount of respect or appreciation for having written this book, but that respect cannot put arms around me when I hurt. The amount of joy that I receive from the love of my children cannot be replaced. It fuels me for coping with life's less satisfying moments. As I attempt to help patients and families prepare for death, I find it important to help them speak the words of love and appreciation that often go unsaid, and that will support them as they move through their time of grief.

Few words are sadder than those heard following a sudden death: "If only I had told her how much I loved her." Sadder yet is the sense of incompleteness and the lack of closure that the omission creates. Because so much of our sense of self-worth is derived from the satisfaction of mutually loving relationships, to fail to say the words that should have been said is to raise questions of the integrity of our own lives. It has been said that "death provokes an identity crisis. When someone we love dies, part of us dies with them."[6]

Third, for some the prospect of death brings with it the threat of separation from God. Our "death appears to indict the Creator, for it raises the question, How did it happen that the undying Creator made life subject to death?"[7] This is particularly present when the death forces doubts about God's power or love. The death of an infant, a tragic suicide, a sudden and wrenching accidental death, raise questions that are unique. When parents lose a child, it is not at all unusual to find their anger directed at the God they had assumed would protect that child. Having lifted their prayers to God for the life of the child to no avail, they may find themselves in sympathy with Albert Camus, who wondered if it "mightn't be better for God if we refuse to believe in Him and struggle with all our might against death, without raising our eyes toward the heaven where He sits in silence."[8]

To nurture such disbelief, however, is to cast our fate to the winds. In every culture, from the beginning of time, there has been some kind of belief in a god who has served as the bulwark against death. The god may have been unreliable or capricious, but it was there and belief in the god was better than facing alone the onslaught of an uncertain future. Nevertheless, it is not unusual today to find members of our congregations opting to do just that, to raise "the question of God's providential participation in what happens to persons when crisis comes."[9] In many quarters, the concept of a god who arrives in the nick of time to deliver us from pain and despair has had to give way to the challenge of those who regard such a belief as demeaning to humans at best, or little more than an "anthropocentric delusion"[10] at worst. The offer of prayer to a patient today may well be met with a comment such as "Why not, it can't hurt!" Clearly, there is no conviction that it can help either.

I have written elsewhere of the need to examine the traditional concept of God's omnipotence which accords God all of the power that exists in the world, thus making him responsible for all that happens to us, and of the need to develop the concept of a vulnerable God who stands with us in the face of death while allowing participation in God's creative activity.[11] If we are to effectively address the challenge of death's threat to separate us from God's providence, there is need for a new vision. There remains wisdom in the advice from Proverbs: "Where there is no vision, the people perish" (29:18, KJV).

The Restoration of Meaning

If many are taking their fate into their own hands today, not all of the ways in which they attempt to deaden the pain are constructive. In his Pulitzer Prize-winning examination of the heroic, Ernest Becker noted that

> modern man is drinking and drugging himself out of awareness, or he spends his time shopping, which is the same thing. As awareness calls for types of heroic dedication that his culture no longer provides for him, society contrives to help him forget. Or alternatively, he buries himself in psychology in the belief that awareness all by itself will be some kind of magical cure for all his problems. But psychology

was born with the breakdown of shared social heroisms; it can only be gone beyond with the creation of new heroisms that are basically matters of belief and will, dedication to a vision.[12]

When all of the heroics have passed, death remains very personally present. It is still *I* who must contemplate death's coming. It is still *I* who must pass alone through death's portal, no matter how much support I receive from those whose love sustains me. To make that passage, I need a vision stronger than my own heroics, a vision stronger than death itself. If death's major impact is at the point of meaning, then it follows that a helpful vision of death is one which seeks to restore that meaning. Vision begins at the point of restoring death's place as a natural part of life.

Ever since Jessica Mitford first broke the ice with *The American Way of Death,* it has become almost commonplace to read accounts of how death is made to seem unreal in our society. Practices ranging from cosmetically attempting to make the dead appear to be asleep to covering the dirt at the grave-site with imitation grass work to remove the sting from death. Our concern to be sensitive to the feelings of persons affects the way we speak about death. Persons no longer die; they expire—like a magazine subscription. I have heard physicians bring word of a death to a family by saying, "I'm sorry; I lost her." Perhaps we can be forgiven for thinking to ourselves, "If you just go back and look around, maybe you'll find her again." And that does not even begin to address

the perhaps unwitting but nonetheless incredible
assumption of responsibility for life on the part of the
physician. But, then, it can be said that "playing God
is the physician's method of augmenting his belief in
his personal specialness."[13]

In contrast to the mortician's cosmetology and the
physician's semantics, the Bible brings a strong
measure of reality to the subject of death. It does not
spare our feelings by making death appear any less
threatening than it is. The writer of Ecclesiastes
reminds us that there is "a time to be born and a time
to die" (3:2). When David sought to prepare his son
for his father's death he said, "I am about to go the
way of all the earth" (I Kings 2:2). In the descriptions
of Jesus' death there is no attempt made by the
gospel writers to make his crucifixion anything other
than what it was: a brutal and dehumanizing
execution.

To be born is to begin life's inexorable march
toward death. The older we become, the more
conscious we are of death around us. We attend class
reunions and immediately notice the persons who
are no longer there. The news media nightly regale
us with tales of the sudden and tragic demise of
persons. With the onset of middle age we find
ourselves scanning the obituaries for names that are
familiar to us. We read the labels of food containers
to weed out carcinogens and cholesterol that can
subject us to death-threatening illnesses. In short,
although death may be the "outermost boundary of
finite existence, even as time, which in its movement
takes us toward death, is the most immediate," there

is no doubt that "to live in time is to live toward death."[14] We are aware of this, no matter how diligently we work to obscure it or distance ourselves from it.

The way to remove death's sting is not to cover it up but to acknowledge it, to own it. The Bible tells us how that is possible. "Even though I walk through the valley of the shadow of death, I fear no evil, for thou art with me" (Ps. 23:4). We do not walk heroically alone. We walk in the presence of the God of Abraham, Isaac, and Jacob, the God made flesh in Jesus Christ. In every moment of life and death, his promise stands, "Lo, I am with you" (Matt. 28:20). I have seen dying persons grasp that vision and be enabled to move confidently toward death in the knowledge that they are not alone.

But there is more. If the first element of our vision restores death to its rightful place as a part of life, it is necessary to modify the way we view death. In a death-denying society, there is need for reminder that "death and life are interdependent. . . . Recognition of death contributes a sense of poignancy to life, provides a radical shift of life perspective, and can transport one from a mode of living characterized by diversions, tranquilization, and petty anxieties to a more authentic mode."[15] Such a view, while giving the heroic its due, also frees us from all of the machinations that we devise to keep death at bay and enables us to live in the face of the inevitable with genuinely faithful courage. In addition, with faith in God's presence to sustain us, we are free to live in very positive fashion, filling our days with all of the meaning that we can find.

This is illustrated in the behavior of patients with whom I minister daily, particularly those patients whose diagnosis involves cancer or heart disease. It is common in the midst of the confrontation with death for patients to examine what have been priorities in their lives and vow to change those priorities in order to achieve greater meaning in their lives. Frequently, this reordering finds work supplanted by family as the most important priority. At such times, I always wish that we did not wait until we are looking through the eyes of our own mortality to make that choice.

Jesus said, "Do not be anxious about tomorrow" (Matt. 6:34). I believe that was his attempt to persuade us to live one day at a time, taking the time each day to love ourselves and our families. In another context Nathan Scott wrote of the mistake that we make when we look at life "sub specie aeternitatis, under the aspect of eternity." From that point of view it is tempting to view our lives as unending and to regard death as something that happens to other people. Rather, we should view our lives "sub specie temporalitatis: subject to the movement of time toward its ending.[16] We should regard each day as a gift from the Author of all time and live it in the knowledge that "neither death nor life . . . nor anything else in all creation will be able to separate us from the love of God in Christ Jesus our Lord" (Rom. 8:38-9).

Notes

1. *The Broken Connection* (New York: Basic Books, 1979), p. 4.
2. *Pilgrim at Tinker Creek* (New York: Bantam Books, 1974), p. 7.
3. See Irvin Yalom, *Existential Psychotherapy* (New York: Basic Books, 1980), pp. 96-133. Yalom develops this sense of specialness as well as the dynamics that take place when the myth of specialness is shattered.
4. *The Death of Ivan Ilyich and Other Stories* (New York: Signet Classics, 1960), pp. 131-32.
5. Charles W. Wahl, "The Fear of Death," in Robert Fulton, ed., *Death and Identity* (New York: John Wiley and Sons, 1965), p. 57.
6. William H. Willimon, *Worship as Pastoral Care* (Nashville: Abingdon Press, 1979), p. 106.
7. Leander E. Keck, "New Testament Views of Death," in Liston O. Mills, ed., *Perspectives on Death* (Nashville: Abingdon, 1969), p. 97.
8. *The Plague,* Stuart Gilbert, trans. (New York: Modern Library, 1948), pp. 117-18.
9. Charles V. Gerkin, *Crisis Experience in Modern Life* (Nashville: Abingdon, 1979), p. 17.
10. *Existential Psychotherapy,* p. 96.
11. Kent D. Richmond, *Preaching to Sufferers: God and the Problem of Pain* (Nashville: Abingdon, 1988).
12. *The Denial of Death* (New York: The Free Press, 1973), p. 284.
13. *Existential Psychotherapy,* p. 133.
14. *Crisis Experience in Modern Life,* p. 74.
15. *Existential Psychotherapy,* p. 40.
16. "The Burdens and Temptations of the Pulpit," in *Preaching on Suffering and a God of Love,* ed. and with a foreword by Henry J. Young (Philadelphia: Fortress, 1978), p. 11.

CHAPTER TWO

The Funeral

The great problem for the survivors in all cultures is to convert "homeless souls," particularly those of the recent dead, into comfortably enshrined or immortalized souls. Funeral ceremonies are rites of passage precisely for this purpose.

ROBERT JAY LIFTON[1]

Against the definition of the purpose of a funeral as being "for the family," I argue that the purpose is the same as for any service of Christian worship: to worship God.

WILLIAM H. WILLIMON[2]

A wise pastor recognizes that a real potential for misunderstanding exists at the beginning of every discussion between the pastor and the bereaved family. As is implied by the title of Edgar N. Jackson's 1963 study of the funeral, *For the Living*, most pastors perceive the service to be of primary benefit to the bereaved family. On the other hand, it has been my experience that most bereaved families view the funeral service as something that they do for the deceased. Then, to complicate choices further, William Willimon advocates the belief that the primary purpose of the funeral, as noted above, is "to worship God." The latter becomes particularly problematic to the family if, as is often the case with some deaths, God is being held to blame for the pain.

The Purpose of the Funeral

The truth, obviously, is that the funeral serves all of the above functions, and the pastor needs to be sensitive to that fact as she goes about the work of planning a service with a bereaved family. W. A. Poovey recognized five functions in the funeral service. Funerals "satisfy the need of people to do something for the dead"; they "help people accept the painful reality of death"; they provide "a time and place for the release of emotions" as well as an opportunity for "community support for the be-reaved." Most important is the context that the funeral provides in which the church can concentrate on the linch-pin of its faith, the Resurrection.[3]

Edgar Jackson's outline seems more focused on the mourners and their emotional dynamics. Jackson wrote that the funeral should "lift the focus of attention from death, tragedy and events . . . not by denying them, but rather by helping to fit them into a larger perspective." Similarly, he felt that the service should "emphasize the elements of a tradition that gives people the long view." Clearly, Jackson was concerned to view death as a natural part of life. He felt that the service should stress "the importance of a living faith that can give courage in the present and direction for the future," provide the opportunity for the expression of "group strength available to the individual who is weakened by sorrow," and "recognize the dignity of life and the validity of the feelings that people feel in the face of death."[4]

In my view the funeral provides a context in which a number of important tasks can be accomplished. There is need on the part of the bereaved survivors to do whatever they can for their loved one. We may say what we will about the exorbitant amounts of money expended (heightened on occasion to assuage someone's feeling of guilt), about the sadness of waiting until the funeral to "say it with flowers," or about the unreality of a situation in which death is made to appear more a nap than nothingness, but the need remains for the survivors to be able to feel that "we did all that we could." Families want a sense of having done "what's right." Moreover, the sense of having done that lends a feeling of completeness to the act, which signals the time for reconstructive grief work to begin. Having done what they can for the deceased, the family now must turn their thoughts to taking care of their own needs.

A second function of the funeral is that of emphasizing the reality of death. It is common for the bereaved to go through the brief period following the death in a state of numbness or shock. They go through the motions, doing what needs to be done, but they carry with them a sense of unreality. "It just can't be" is a comment often voiced.

With the coming of the funeral, however, the reality of death is set indelibly into the consciousness

of families. Cosmetology notwithstanding, there is
just no way to deny the presence of the body in the
casket and the unmistakable message that it
communicates.

A third function of the funeral is that of providing a
context for the expression of grief. In a society where
weeping may be seen as communicating anything
from weakness—particularly with males—to hys-
teria, there is a sense of permissiveness about the
funeral that enables the shedding of tears. "It's O.K.
to cry here" is the message communicated, no doubt
reflecting our common feeling of being defenseless
in the face of death. Weeping is a healthy release of
emotion that facilitates the process of grieving. I
suspect that we cannot begin to grieve for someone
until we have wept for him.

A fourth function of the funeral is that of providing
a place where friends and relatives from the
community can express their support to the
bereaved family. By enabling this expression to take
place, the bereaved family provides a ministry of
their own to the community. There is a *need* on the
part of friends of the family to express their sorrow
and the desire to provide whatever support that they
can for the family of the deceased. This need is every
bit as real as the stricken family's need for
community support. Thomas C. Oden wrote meaningfully of the funeral of his father. What he
remembered were the many ways of caring expressed by those who came and the personal nature
of their remembrances of his father. Because it was

Christmastime, the kind remembrances brought
home to him the meaning of the season.[5]

Finally, the funeral is a means through which the
church can bring God's word of life. There, in the
almost tangible presence of death, the reality of the
Resurrection comes with power. We may express
our faith in God's gift of the Resurrection on
occasions throughout the church year, but at no time
does it come with such relevance as in the funeral
service. At no other time are we as able to hear it, as
open to its promise, nor as willing to consider its
meaning and call to responsible discipleship. At
almost every funeral there will be those in
attendance whose lives do not include relationships
to a church, let alone attendance at worship. The
funeral provides the pastor a context in which to
share with these people a word that they need to
hear—a word that can shift the focus of their lives
from death to life, from weeping to joy. Resurrection
proclaims to us the happy word that "weeping may
tarry for the night, but joy comes with the morning"
(Ps. 30:5).

The Order and Conduct of the Funeral

Unless the pastor is called to be with a family at the
time of the death of their loved one, word of the
death almost always come from the mortician rather
than the family. That is a bit like receiving word of an
up-coming wedding by being notified that a hall has
been rented for the reception. I have always
appreciated the families who, at a time of death,

think first of calling the pastor. That enables me to be
with them from the very beginning, before any
arrangements have been made. Perhaps if we
prepared the ground ourselves by preaching on
death as part of our regular Sunday worship this
practice might be changed.

Because of time constraints, discussion of the
funeral arrangements with the family should begin as
soon as possible. Usually, this should take place at
the pastor's first meeting with the family following
word of the death. To avoid the impersonality that
strangely marks some services, the family should be
asked about favorite hymns, passages of scripture,
poetry, and so forth that will make the service more
meaningful for them.

A family should not be led to believe that
everything they submit will find its way into the
service. Many pastors have done so only to have the
family present them with material clearly inappropriate to the setting. A simple statement by the
pastor to the effect that she will *try* to use the
material, but can't promise to use all of it, usually
serves to avoid this potential problem. On the only
occasion in my ministry in which this became a
problem, the matter was resolved by allowing the
family to present the questionable material after I
had concluded the service.

Whenever possible and appropriate, funeral
services should be conducted in the church.
Certainly this should be the practice for those who
have been faithful members. At the first meeting
with the family, I try to point out the advantages of

this. The entire mood of the service is changed when the service is conducted in the sanctuary. The presence of organ and hymnals facilitates congregational participation. All of the appointments, from the stained glass to the colors in paraments and pall, help to shift the focus from the casket in the front to the promises of God. All of our senses are involved in a way that just is not possible in the sterile environs of the funeral home.

Morticians, however, do not provide those nice "memory rooms" and "parlors" with the intention that they not be used. Occasionally a mortician will resist moving the casket with the remains to the church for the service. Unfortunately, many charge a transportation fee for the service. In my experience, however, their own faith and church involvement has moved them to attempt to be as helpful as possible.

In the area in which I have been a pastor, it is the custom for the mortician to bring the casket to the church about two to three hours in advance of the service and to allow an hour or two of viewing and visiting by those who have been unable to go to the funeral home the previous night. This should be done in a smaller room in the church or in the narthex. In smaller churches it may not be possible to view anywhere other than in the sanctuary, but this should be avoided if at all possible. The sanctuary should be preserved as the place for worship of God and for the change of focus from death to life.

Practice varies with regard to whether the

bereaved family watches the closing of the casket. If the family has been able to approach the service with a measure of calm, watching the casket lid close over their loved one may be all that is necessary to move them to uncontrolled weeping. Others feel that witnessing the closing adds a measure of finality to the service. It has been my preference to have the casket closed privately prior to the service. This assists the pastor in her attempt to help the mourners shift their focus from the death represented by the casket to the promise of new life that is at the heart of the service and the sermon.

After the casket has been closed, it should be covered by a pall. The pall is a symbol that does more than cover the casket and its brand name. It is a symbol representing our having been baptized into Christ's fellowship and, at the time of death, being covered by the grace of God as we move toward God's gift of life.

The pastor precedes the casket into the sanctuary; the family follows the casket. The congregation remains standing until all are in place and the casket has reached the bottom of the chancel stairs, outside the communion rail. There it will remain through the service. It has been suggested that the casket be carried by the pall-bearers to this point, rather than wheeled in on a cart.[6] In reality, however, most sanctuary aisles are too narrow to permit this.

There are many different orders for the burial of the dead readily available. Denominational books of worship are mines of resources for liturgical use. There are also books of materials specifically aimed at

use within the funeral service.[7] For most of my
ministry I have used the rather "bare bones" service
provided in my own United Methodist *Book of
Worship*. The last decade, however, has seen a
renewed interest in worship and a concomitant
development of new forms of liturgy, which give a
refreshing richness to worship today. The Supplemental Worship Resources series issued by The
United Methodist Church is one example. In this
series, *A Service of Death and Resurrection* brings
an especially rich experience to those who mourn.[8]

Regardless of the order used, it should work to "lift
the focus of attention from death . . . not by denying
(it) but rather by helping to fit [it] into a larger
perspective"[9]: God's word of life in Jesus Christ.
With that effort in mind, the service should be as
personal as possible for the bereaved family. I have
attended funeral services in which it seemed that the
order of worship could have been lifted out and
placed in the context of any other person's funeral. I
have heard families later express their wonder as to
whether the pastor even knew the deceased. Paul
Irion has emphasized the importance of "maximum
participation" by the mourners in the funeral
service.[10]

There are many ways that this participation can be
achieved. The initial visit with the family provides
resources that can be included in the sermon or
liturgy. The use of a bulletin involves the congregation in the prayers and responses. The writing of
prayers and selecting of scripture passages that relate
to the life of the deceased are very helpful. The

family may place the pall over the casket prior to the service. Two elements, the "Naming" and the "Witness," contained in *A Service of Death and Resurrection* also are very helpful.[11] Similar to a eulogy, the "Naming" provides a place for the pastor to present a brief account of the life of the deceased. The "Witness" provides opportunity for family members or others to offer brief words of thanksgiving for the life of the deceased.

Hymns or other music can help to involve the congregation in the worship as well as to make it more personal for the family. Pastors probably encounter more difficulty selecting hymns, however, than at any other point of preparation for the worship. Such hymns as "In the Garden" and "Nearer My God to Thee" continue to be perennial favorites, despite their rather shallow theology and tendency to be maudlin. When possible, without being adamant, the pastor can try to help families consider hymns such as "Praise to the Lord, the Almighty" and "Now Thank We All Our God." These hymns offer thanksgiving to the greatness of God, "who, from our mother's arms, has blessed us on our way with countless gifts of love, And still is ours today."[12]

When the hymn is to be sung by a soloist, it is a simple matter to place the solo ahead of the sermon so that the pastor has the opportunity to shift the focus if necessary. Sometimes, however, we simply have to reconcile ourselves to the use of hymns that we would rather not sing in the interest of preserving an on-going opportunity for ministry to the bereaved family.

At the conclusion of the service, the pastor should precede the casket out of the sanctuary. At the cemetery, the pastor again precedes the casket to its resting place over the grave. The committal service should be brief, may or may not use earth as a symbol of the earth to which we return, and should emphasize the committing of the deceased to God's care. On occasion, I have invited family members and friends to share briefly a few of their good memories of the deceased. Such a practice has seemed particularly appropriate when there has been no funeral service and the pastor is asked to meet with the family only for a private committal.

Ministry Following the Funeral

In the weeks following the funeral, ministry to the mourners must continue. Grieving can be a lengthy process, characteristically lasting in excess of a year. We all have encountered the grieving family member who has held up "like a brick" through the whole process to the marvel of friends and the concern of family. When a family has gone through a long terminal illness with a loved one, much anticipatory grieving may take place in advance of the death. Family members may be "cried out" by the time death comes. On the other hand, a mourner may be trying valiantly to hold emotions in check in the belief that it is best to be strong for the sake of others in the family. In the weeks that follow, the pastor may be instrumental in helping such persons to express the grief that they have been repressing. In my work as a hospital chaplain, it is not unusual to encounter patients who bring unresolved grief of some years' duration to their confinement. When these feelings are not released, they can become the source of later illness.[13]

I have made a habit of calling on the bereaved family one week after the funeral and at two-week to monthly intervals until the most intense grieving seems to have passed. Thereafter, occasional calls seem to be helpful until the family appears to be well on the road to recovering from their grief. When possible, special attention should be paid to dates such as anniversaries, birthdays, or holidays that have held special meaning for the family. Such care on the part of the pastor can lead to a deeply meaningful relationship with the bereaved family.

Special Problems

A few special considerations remain to be examined. Without proper preparation and sensitive handling, these considerations have the potential to become painful stumbling blocks to the pastor. Military and fraternal rites, for example, can present a challenge to the pastor. Fraternal rites seem less directed at the praise and thanksgiving of God than at eulogizing the deceased's participation in the order. Some denominations are adamant about these rites having "no place within the service of the church."[14] When a family has deemed such rites important, I

have requested that the rites be held either the night
before or the hour before the Christian funeral
service. At the cemetery, however, the presence of
the flag-draped casket, the salute, and the playing of
taps can lend a deeply impressive tone to the
committal.

Recent years have seen an increased incidence of
private memorial services. Private services are held
most often in relation to deaths that seem to have
brought a feeling of shame or embarrassment to the
family. Suicide, for example, may cause the
survivors of the deceased to feel that the less contact
they have with people, the easier the experience will
be. In reality, the family is denying itself the very
community support that can help it grieve effectively.

> As more is learned about handling bereave-
> ment . . . most psychiatric personnel who help
> grieving families have come to view the private
> service with disfavor. [Most often such families] feel
> shame compounded with their grief. . . . It would
> appear to me that *they*—almost more than other
> bereaved—need every bit of loving and caring and
> kindness that can be offered by friends and
> acquaintances.[15]

Memorial services, on the other hand, mark the
passing of a life in a context in which the body is not
present. Increasingly, as cremation is chosen as the
means of disposing of the remains and as bodies are
donated to medical institutions, this form of service
has become more common. The service differs little

from the funeral that it replaces. The casket may be replaced by a photograph or portrait of the deceased. Often taking place a week or more after the death, the service allows more time to the pastor for preparation.

More problematic are services that the pastor is asked to conduct for persons who had little or no relationship to the church prior to death. Most pastors, particularly if living in a smaller community, have been called to conduct the funeral of someone's "dear old Uncle Harry," who never darkened the door of a church in his life. Some denominations simply refuse to conduct services for the un- churched. In the early years of my ministry, I served a church in a small community where ours was the only church that did not have such a policy. As a result, I was called to preside at the funerals of all of the persons that the other two clergypersons in the community would not accept.

I vividly remember the morning a young couple appeared tearfully at the parsonage to ask me to conduct the funeral for her father. They had been to see their own pastor, who had refused the service because the deceased had not been in "active" membership in his church. I have long believed that everyone deserves a decent burial, no matter how her or his life was lived, and that when it comes to the matter of evaluating a person's life, God is much better equipped to do that than we are. I assured the couple that I would "bury" her father. At a local clergy meeting not long after, I remember the couple's pastor expressing his bewilderment at the number of his younger members who seemed to be attending worship at the church I was serving.

More difficult is the occasion on which the pastor is asked to preside at the funeral for a person who has no relationship to any church or person in the community. In the interests of decency and out of the belief that God is the ultimate judge of our lives, I have never refused one of these services. Agreeing to perform these services also helps the pastor's relationship with the local mortician, who shares the desire to aid the bereaved.

Probably most difficult of all services is the funeral for a person known to be a real reprobate. It is rare to find someone about whom no one can say anything worthwhile, but it does happen. Again, I have accepted such funerals, but I have been frank about the character of the life lived. It is possible on such an occasion to remind the congregation that we are not called by God to judge the quality of a life and we should live with a realistic understanding that "There, but for the grace of God, I go."

Whether conducting a funeral or memorial service, pastors need to remember that they are called by God to confront squarely the mystery of suffering and death. That confrontation extends to those gathered for the service. The service reminds all of us that we cannot live with the illusion that death is something that happens to other people—that God will somehow protect us from death's inevitability. At the same time, however, when we honestly confront the reality of death, it is in that moment that liberation begins. We are freed from the fear of death and opened to the assurance of God's word of resurrection. At no other point in our ministry are Jesus' words of life heard with more eagerness. "I came that they may have life, and have it abundantly" (John 10:10). It is our unique challenge to proclaim that gift of life, not only in terms of "kairos," God's time, but also as present possibility in "chronos," our time. Whereas the Resurrection removes the sting of death by pointing us in the direction of God's eternity, it also bids us to see God's life-giving presence in the persons and events that resurrect us in our mourning. Even though the hymns and prayers, the scripture, and the support of other persons that are part of the funeral help to contribute toward that meaning, at no point is there greater opportunity for the pastor to speak of what he believes than as he delivers the sermon.

Notes

1. *The Broken Connection* (New York: Basic Books, 1979), p. 95.
2. *Worship as Pastoral Care* (Nashville: Abingdon, 1979), p. 115.
3. *Planning a Christian Funeral* (Minneapolis: Augsburg, 1978), pp. 11-17.
4. *For the Living* (Des Moines: Channel Press, 1963), p. 79.
5. "My Dad's Death Brought Christmas Home," *Christianity Today* (Dec. 11, 1981): pp. 20-22.
6. The General Board of Discipleship of The United Methodist Church, *A Service of Death and Resurrection: The Ministry of the Church at Death* (Nashville: Abingdon, 1979), p. 46.

7. See, for example, Perry H. Biddle, Jr., *The Abingdon Funeral Manual* (Nashville: Abingdon, 1976, rev. 1984); Al Cadenhead, Jr., *The Minister's Manual for Funerals* (Nashville: Broadman, 1988); Friedrich Rest, *Funeral Handbook* (Valley Forge, Pa.: Judson, 1985).

8. The order can be found along with commentary in *A Service of Death and Resurrection: The Ministry of the Church at Death.*

9. *For the Living.*

10. *The Funeral: Vestige or Value?* (Nashville: Abingdon, 1966), p. 172. It has even been suggested that mourners can become involved to some degree in the work of the mortician. See, e.g., Elisabeth Kübler-Ross, *Death, the Final Stage of Growth* (Englewood Cliffs, N.J.: Prentice-Hall, 1975), pp. 87-96.

11. See p. x of the service, and pp. 58-61 of the commentary in *A Service of Death and Resurrection.*

12. "Now Thank We All Our God," *The United Methodist Hymnal* (Nashville: The United Methodist Publishing House, 1989), p. 102.

13. See Richard G. Bruehl, "Mourning, Family Dynamics, and Pastoral Care" in *Death and Ministry,* ed. Donald J. Bane, Austin H. Kutscher, Robert E. Neale, Robert B. Reeves (New York: Seabury, 1975), pp. 92-101.

14. *The Lutheran Book of Worship* (Minneapolis: Augsburg, 1978), p. 206.

15. Harriet Sarnoff Schiff, *The Bereaved Parent* (New York: Crown, 1977), p. 12.

CHAPTER THREE

The Funeral Sermon

The preacher must remember that he is not a mere eulogist of the dead, but only adds this task to his work of preaching the gospel. Accordingly, his utterances as to the departed . . . must be *scrupulously true*, though not necessarily *all* the truth.
JOHN A. BROADUS[1]

The writer does not recommend a return to the practise of preaching at a funeral.
ANDREW WATTERSON BLACKWOOD[2]

How are they to hear without a preacher?
PAUL, ROMANS 10:14

Preaching has not always taken place at a funeral. When John A. Broadus delivered his Lyman Beecher lectures at Yale University in 1888–89, the practice of preaching at a funeral was common. Half a century later, no less a homiletic crafts-person than Andrew Blackwood advised against a return to the practice. Blackwood's advice sprang from his belief that few pastors took the time to properly prepare and deliver the funeral sermon.[3] It also could be argued, however, that there has been little in print to

45

guide pastors in the preparation and delivery of the
funeral sermon. The two volumes that have helped
train main-line denomination pastors in the latter
half of this century contain no advice with regard to
preaching in this difficult context.[4] The difficulty of
such preaching is better understood after considering the elements that make the funeral service
unique.

The Marks of Uniqueness

Time may seem to be the enemy when a pastor
prepares for a funeral. Whereas the pastor has a week
to prepare the Sunday sermon, she generally has
from one to three days to prepare for a funeral. When
a pastor has two or three funerals in a week, in
addition to the Sunday sermon, she may begin to
wonder if she chose the right profession!

In addition to the time bind, the nature of the
congregation is unique. There will be persons
present out of respect for the deceased who would
not otherwise be found in church. Some will come
from other denominations and will bring different or
even conflicting theological meanings to their
hearing of the sermon. I remember a woman who, at
the conclusion of a service I conducted for a person of
another denomination, expressed her reluctant
praise for the service as well as her sense of sadness
that the bereaved family had found it necessary to
"get a Methodist to do it!"

The setting may be unique as well. Many services
are held in the funeral home rather than the church.

In such cases, the pastor cannot count upon the support of organ, hymnals, or symbolic surroundings that assist the mourners in focusing upon God's promise of life. In areas where it is customary for the casket to remain open during the service, the pastor may feel himself struggling to pull the congregation's attention from the casket to the sermon.

Two elements of uniqueness assist the pastor. One is the length of the sermon. The funeral service is brief; the sermon is even shorter. Eight to twelve minutes is a good length for the sermon. To preach much longer than that creates the risk of saying more than can be retained by the listeners. David Buttrick reminds us that there is some "indication now that audience attention span is brief—not much more than four minutes to a single conceptual idea."[5] Care must be taken to carefully craft the sermon so that what must be said can be contained within the brief time allotted.

Finally, there is no other pastoral context in which the pastor experiences a congregation so open to ministry, so willing to hear what is said. The funeral offers such potential for the building of relationships that I am saddened every time I hear of one that was poorly done. The dynamics of grief are such that the bereaved can be eager to hear the Resurrection's message of continuing life in the light of God's love. To fail to bring that message is tragic; to offer it, on the other hand, is to know the gratitude of a family that will continue to sustain a pastor throughout her ministry. With so much at stake, let us look at the elements that go into the preparation of the funeral sermon.

Personal Death-Awareness

Preparation for the sermon begins long before the pastor enters her study. Henri Nouwen noted that the pastor's "service will not be perceived as authentic unless it comes from a heart wounded by the suffering about which" she speaks.[6] That authenticity starts to develop when the pastor first begins to be aware of her own mortality and of the feelings born from that discovery.

I remember my own anxiety when I first responded to a family's request to be with them at a time of death. Previous experiences of death in my own family had not sufficiently prepared me for the starkness of the body in the bed. "It" was the person that I had known, and yet "it" was not. The alien awkwardness of the situation was not made easier by the flood of uncertainty that I experienced in my pastoral role, and the awareness of vulnerability and mortality that came to me personally. That I would constantly step in and out of similar situations throughout the years of my ministry did not occur to me. If it had, I might have questioned my adequacy for pastoral ministry. One thought was foremost in my mind: "Some day that's going to happen to me." With that thought came a small measure of understanding of what the bereaved family was feeling.

What I was experiencing has been called death

awareness, and it comes to us in several forms.[7] One of these is the awareness of finitude. The intensity of this experience is determined by age. Youth's involvement in aspirations, in hopes and dreams about the future, and in the myth of immortality causes this awareness to come to them with more force than it does to the aged who may feel that they have lived long and well.

Another element in death awareness might be called "ordinariness." It is the realization that we are no different than the other millions of people in the world. We are like grains of sand on a beach. When the waves wash us away, billions of others will remain, filling in the space that we occupied. Life will go on without us. It may seem to some as if they never lived.

A third element in death awareness, which is closely related to "ordinariness," can be identified as the loss of our sense of specialness. Specialness is born in the belief that God will protect us from pain and suffering. When this belief is exploded, it in turn can force us to reexamine what we believe about God. Such reexamination often, but not always, leads to a stronger faith. For others, reexamination brings a feeling of betrayal.

Powerlessness is yet another way that death awareness comes to us. Nothing so upsets our applecart as that which is beyond our control. To know that something will happen to us regardless of what we wish or do may cause us to abandon hope. It also can bring us to live one day at a time, packing each day full of meaning.

The Purpose of the Funeral Sermon

Coming to grips with the knowledge that we will die helps us to understand the purposes of the funeral sermon. The sermon must provide an answer to three questions that are present in the minds of the bereaved: (1) Will the deceased be cared for? (2) Will the survivors be cared for? (3) What word does God speak in the face of death?

Concern for the well-being of the deceased is foremost in the minds of the bereaved. The sense of anxiety is heightened in those who have cared for their loved one during a long period of illness before his death. The concern for well-being may take other forms such as, "Will he get into heaven?" or "Who will care for her now that I can no longer do it?" If the death has been particularly sudden, unexpected, or tragic, it may raise questions related to God's omnipotence or love. When a child dies, many wonder what it means for a life to have been given so briefly. Given the deep parental need to protect and defend their children, a sermon that focuses upon Jesus' love for little children can help parents feel that their child is cared for even though she is beyond their embrace.

"Will the survivors be cared for?" is the question of grief. I have heard people who are trying to cope with grief wonder if their lives ever will be the same again. The answer to that question may be "No, it won't, but with God's help you may be able to experience both life and death in a deeper, more reflective manner."

An understanding of the symptoms of grief is helpful to the pastor who would assist families as they journey through the pain. Numerous authors have noted the classic dynamics of grief.[8] Grief begins with a sense of shock. Persons may shake their heads in disbelief. Feeling numb, they may remark, "It just can't be." Shock may be followed by catharsis, or the out-pouring of emotion. Like a dam that has suddenly given way to the pressure of a flood, the tears may suddenly flow. Depression may follow when the reality of death finally sets in. There may be expressions of guilt by those who feel that they were somehow responsible for the death or wish that they had told the deceased how much they loved her. There may be preoccupation with the loss. Those closest to the deceased may find his death to be the only thing that they can think about and wonder if they are losing their sanity. Late in the process may come a time of anger, often directed at God or even at the pastor who may be seen as God's representative. Finally, perhaps one or two years after the death, a sense of acceptance may finally dawn.

The bereaved may not go through all of these stages, and the order of the stages may be different. For example, family members who have spent a long period caring for a person with a terminal illness may have already done much anticipatory grieving and may experience the death with a sense of relief or release. Others may grieve as if they have been separated from life itself.[9] Whatever the degree of intensity, those who mourn require the assurance that they *will* survive the pain. Though they may never be totally free of hurt, that hurt can serve to strengthen and even enable them to find blessings in the experience of loss.

The third question regarding God's involvement in the experience of death and bereavement may be the easiest or the most difficult of the questions to answer. A solid presentation of God's response to death in Jesus' resurrection may be all that is needed to minister to the needs of some, particularly persons mourning the death of an elderly person whose long life was full and faithful. On the other hand, the tragic suicide of a teen-aged boy can raise issues such as why God did not protect the boy or enable the parents to recognize the possibility of the act. The Bible assures us that not a sparrow falls to the ground escaping God's notice (Matt. 10:49), but it does not tell us why *one* sparrow falls rather than another.

These questions must be aired before we can respond in terms of what God promises to those who suffer and die. Only the assurance of God's on-going love and care for the deceased and his peace and support for those who mourn can provide us with the strength to pick up the pieces of our lives.

It may seem to many that the ultimate require-ment—to give up one's self and one's life—repre-sents a kind of cruelty on the part of God or fate, which makes our existence a sort of bad joke which can never be accepted. This attitude is particularly true in present-day Western culture, in which the self is held sacred and death is considered an unspeakable insult. Yet the exact opposite is the reality. It is in the giving up of self that human beings can find the most ecstatic and lasting, solid, durable joy of life. And it is death that provides life with all its meaning.[10]

On the edge of his own death Jesus said, "Father, into thy hands I commit my spirit" (Luke 23:46), knowing that God had promised him life made more rich and full by virtue of its being lived in the light of God's presence. To those of us who follow him, he has renewed God's offer. In the face of all pain and grief he speaks the words we need most to hear, promising not only to receive our spirits but to stand with us in our pain: "Lo, I am with you" (Matt. 28:20).

The Preparation of the Sermon

Many of the steps in the preparation of the funeral sermon are similar to those taken in preparation for the weekly message; however, a few are uniquely tailored to the emotionally charged atmosphere of the funeral. The process begins with the visit to the bereaved family immediately after being notified of the death. As I help them plan the funeral, I always ask a question such as this: "When you think about (the deceased), what things come to mind as being most important about (her or him)?" Initially, the question may be difficult for the family to answer. Usually, however, after the initial hesitation has passed, family members are more than willing to share good memories. Some of these memories can be included in the sermon to make the message

personal for the family. When I am asked to preside
at the funeral of someone previously unknown to me,
this gathering of information is vital.

> There are many funerals which give no clue to
> whether the person who is being buried was young
> or old, male or female. To God and to those who
> grieve, that person was a very special and infinitely
> precious individual. To mark the close of that life
> with a standardized all-purpose service does not
> seem adequate.[11]

Some of the memories that the family shares will
be humorous. If the humorous incident is appropriate, it can be included in the sermon. In a context so
marked by gloom, humor can help to relieve the
tension and to add a sense of normalcy. The Bible
tells us that laughter is a normal part of life. There is
"a time to weep, and a time to laugh" (Eccles. 3:4).

Care must be taken when using humor. The
humorous incident must be respectful of the
deceased. There are deaths that are violent and
unexpected, marked with a particularly strong sense
of tragedy in which laughter is inappropriate.
Suicidal deaths require a more restrained approach.
Good judgment is the rule.

With the personal reminiscences in hand, there
are three additional kinds of material that contribute
to the sermon. Often there are themes that mark the
life of the deceased. What was her life like? Was it
particularly lonely? Was he a loyal member of the
congregation who spent many hours involved in

church work? Was she a person who experienced great moments of joy in ministry to others?

I remember the sense of fulfillment that came to one of my lay leaders who attended a lay-preaching school and later became one of the most sought-after speakers in our district. At first, the thought of preaching a sermon petrified him; however, the more involved he became and the harder he worked at it, the more joy he experienced. Convinced that God was using him to bring a message about the ministry of the laity, he found his faith enlarged and his life enriched. When he died very unexpectedly in the prime of his life, I felt the hurt deeply. His funeral sermon was one of the most difficult I have ever delivered. It focused upon the meaning of friendship as he had lived it in his own ministry—a theme so much a part of his life that it could not be overlooked.

In addition to personal information and themes that were a part of the deceased's life, another block of material to be added to the sermon is derived from questions that are a part of the death itself. Such questions, unless they are addressed, have an intensity that can prevent an audience from hearing anything the pastor says. Some people feel that the subject of suicide is better left unmentioned in a sermon. We can be certain that the subject is present in the minds of our hearers, some of whom are wondering how the pastor will address it. If suicide is dealt with sensitively from the start, it can be set aside and the door can be opened for hope to speak in the face of the despair. Infant death also may raise questions related to God's providence and life's meaning. When the pastor ignores these issues, it may appear to his hearers that his Gospel is not strong enough to stand in the face of such despair. Allowing these questions to speak their words of doubt and anger helps the congregation to remain open to the pastor's assertion that nothing in all of life "will be able to separate us from the love of God in Christ Jesus our Lord" (Rom. 8:39).

A fourth block of sermon material comes from the Bible. After identifying personal memories, themes that are part of the deceased's life, and questions that belong to the context of the service, the search is begun for scriptural passages that bring God's word of life to the sermon. Scripture may relate to the sermon in several ways.

The relationship of the scripture to the sermon material may be complementary, filling out or adding to the previously gathered material. The parable of the widow's mite relates naturally to the death of a widow who freely gave of herself in service to the church and adds a sense of Jesus' approval to her life and ministry (Mark 12:41-44). The parable of the talents may relate in the same manner (Matt. 25:14-29).

The relationship may be one in which the scripture answers a question or provides a solution to a dilemma that is part of the context. Persons who feel that God has abandoned them in their grief or who direct their anger at God may take comfort in knowing that the psalmist stood in their place before them (Ps. 22:1-2).

A third relationship may be one of reinforcement through which the scripture adds strength to what family members already believe about the life of the deceased or about God's promises. After a long and painful terminal illness, families often have a deep desire for relief—for a better life for the deceased. Revelation 21:4 speaks of the author's belief that God "will wipe away every tear from their eyes, and death shall be no more, neither shall there be mourning nor crying nor pain."

The Bible may relate to the sermon in dialectical fashion, providing the synthesis that resolves an apparent deadlock between thesis and antithesis. Jesus spoke of coming to bring us abundant life (John 10:10), but the life of the deceased may have seemed so devoid of abundance as to make Jesus' promise seem questionable. In such a situation, a synthesis might serve to remind us that life is sometimes known more deeply under want or pain. Paul spoke of his own misfortunes and pain, yet he noted that "when I am weak, then I am strong" (II Cor. 12:10).

One of the members of a congregation I served contracted polio at a young age and spent the rest of his life confined to a wheelchair. There were times when his life seemed so difficult as to make any kind of happiness improbable, let alone allow anyone to characterize it as being abundant. Yet, not only did he triumph over the pain, but he spent his life and resources bringing life to others whose pain he well knew for having walked in their shoes. He would have been among the first to have asked, "Lord, when did (I) see thee hungry and feed thee, or thirsty

and give thee drink?" (Matt. 25:37). To all of us who
knew this individual, however, Jesus' invitation
seemed to be spoken especially to him. "Come, O
blessed of my Father, inherit the kingdom prepared
for you" (Matt. 25:34).

When biblical passages are carefully related to the
themes and questions identified, the Bible can have
a relevance and the sermon an urgency that grips and
holds the congregation with an unanticipated drama.
Absolutely central to this result is a word that draws
together all of the sermon material: "brooding."

The word "brooding" brings to mind several
images.[12] It suggests a hen sitting patiently upon a
clutch of eggs. It carries a sense of heavy dwelling
upon a difficult subject. It conjures up images of
someone meditating deeply and reflectively upon an
absorbing subject. *All* of these meanings are
appropriate to the process. Brooding is the quiet,
deep struggling that the pastor must do in the
attempt to understand and be grasped by all of the
meanings contained in the sermon material.

Even the heavy, gloomy sense is appropriate to
sermon construction. In the case of a difficult or
tragic death, the pastor needs to have an experience
of the gloom that the survivors are feeling. Brooding
bids me to try putting myself in the shoes of those
who are feeling the pain. It moves me to enter as far
as I am able into the thoughts of the one who has
died. It asks me to feel the same need for decision on
the part of those who first heard Jesus speak the
words of new life. When Jesus said to his cultured
despisers, "Unless you turn and become like

children, you will never enter the kingdom of heaven" (Matt. 18:3), what went through their minds? How did they feel?

Brooding forces me to reflect, associate, relate, incarnate, and contrast, my way through the material that has been amassed, and to do it with pen in hand. Every thought or feeling that comes to my experience with regard to the material goes down on paper, no matter how irrelevant it may seem. Later exegesis of the scripture resource chosen as a text for the sermon will help to reveal what is irrelevant or incorrect. Often it is through this process of brooding over the material that the most striking associations, meanings, or relationships are revealed. In the quiet struggle that marks this process, God's Spirit is allowed to speak and the sermon is born. It is not too much to suggest that brooding is the difference between a sermon that simply communicates and a message that becomes a language-event in the lives of those who listen. When a message becomes a language-event, God's word may speak with the same force felt by those who first heard Jesus' words.

The remaining steps in building the sermon are similar to those marking the construction of any carefully crafted message. The Biblical passage selected as the text for the sermon must be checked exegetically to ensure that foreign meanings are not imposed upon it. The material must be organized around an outline that clearly carries the preacher from introduction to conclusion. The manuscript should be written out word for word, *even if* the pastor preaches from outline or by rote. There is a discipline in writing sermons that serves the pastor in a number of ways. Writing the sermon helps the pastor to see the movement in the sermon, or the lack of it; to record all of his thoughts on paper and to delete those that seem wordy or tangential; and to carefully select words or phrases on the basis of their illustrative or evocative power.

Finally, the sermon should be practiced a number of times. Familiarity with the material frees the pastor from the manuscript, allowing her to measure the sermon's impact upon the congregants. Since most funeral homes do not have public address systems, familarity with the material enables the pastor to concentrate on the articulation and projection that will assist the congregation in hearing what she has to say.

If the pastor is faithful in working through the steps of sermon preparation, his preaching will be the vehicle of sermon preparation, his preaching will be the vehicle through which God enables healing to take place. After conducting the funeral for a young man who died under very sudden and tragic circumstances, his sister approached me and said, "I didn't think I would ever be able to pray to God again, but you've helped me to see it in a different way." A pastor cannot receive greater praise! Funeral sermons are not easy to prepare or deliver, but when thoughtfully done they can become one of the keys to a fruitful ministry marked by deep, caring relationships.

Notes

1. *A Treatise on the Preparation and Delivery of Sermons* (New York: A. C. Armstrong & Son, 1898), pp. 101-2.
2. *The Funeral* (Philadelphia: Westminster, 1941), p. 134.
3. Ibid.
4. Ilion T. Jones, *Principles and Practise of Preaching* (New York: Abingdon, 1956), and Henry Grady Davis, *Design for Preaching* (Philadelphia: Fortress, 1958).
5. *Homiletic: Moves and Structures* (Philadelphia: Fortress, 1987), p. 26.
6. *The Wounded Healer* (New York: Doubleday Image Books, 1979), p. xvi.
7. I am indebted to Irvin D. Yalom who has an enlarged treatment of these and other characteristics of personal death awareness in his *Existential Psychotherapy* (New York: Basic Books, 1980), pp. 120ff.
8. See, for example, Granger E. Westberg's helpful little book, *Good Grief* (Philadelphia: Fortress, 1971). The symptoms of abnormal grief can be found in Erich Lindemann's classic treatment, "Symptomatology and Management of Acute Grief," in *Pastoral Psychology*, XIV 36 (Sept. 1963): pp. 8-18.
9. David K. Switzer has theorized that all experiences of the death of emotionally significant persons recall the separation anxiety of childhood. See his volume, *The Dynamics of Grief* (Nashville: Abingdon, 1970).
10. W. Scott Peck, *The Road Less Traveled* (New York: Simon and Schuster, 1978), p. 72.
11. George E. Sweazey, *Preaching the Good News* (Englewood Cliffs, N.J.: Prentice-Hall, 1976), p. 277.
12. I am indebted to the late Dr. George A. Buttrick for this concept.

CHAPTER FOUR

Preaching on Difficult Occasions

> One life is not to be evaluated in terms of another life. The goodness of one life is not greater because the goodness in another life is less . . . The fulfillment in one life does not depend on, nor is it to be measured by, the fulfillment in another life.
>
> JACOB PHILIP RUDIN[1]

> Even the most tragic death in the most unpleasant circumstances cannot deny us the possibility of saying thank you to God for something.
>
> IAN BUNTING[2]

Kara was a bright, vivacious seventeen-year-old woman who was looking forward to attending her senior prom. Eager to try the new twelve-speed bicycle she had received for her birthday, she went for a ride in a nearby forest preserve on a beautiful spring day. As she left the house she said, "See you later, Mom," but she never returned. Her battered body was found by a jogger along a lonely trail. The death of someone so young, whose life showed so much promise, made her funeral one of the most difficult services ever conducted by her rabbi.

The enormity of death leaves us speechless at such

tragic times. Although death is always untimely, the force of death varies according to circumstances and the age of the deceased. When death comes to someone who has suffered a long terminal illness, friends and family experience a sense of relief to see their loved one's pain brought to an end. When a young mother dies, leaving a husband and young children without her love and guidance, death brings a sense of injustice and anger. When death comes to a young person such as Kara, the shock is so great that we scarcely can believe that it has happened, let alone know what to say or feel.

Whenever I am asked to officiate at such a funeral, I find myself dealing with many different feelings. I feel an awed sense of humility at being allowed to enter the family's life and pain, and I find myself dealing with my own sense of anger at the unjust and absurd turns that life takes. I experience a sense of inadequacy as I wonder what I can possibly say that will help to ease the pain. A lingering feeling of sadness and a sense of being emotionally drained frequently remain with me after the funeral.

The sermons that follow were written for such occasions. In almost every case, death came suddenly, unexpectedly, and in some cases violently. Each sermon is preceded by an analysis of theological or psychological questions or issues that may be present in the death to which each sermon is addressed. Alternate scriptural texts, commentary on the text selected for the sermon, and additional readings are offered in the hope that the reader will be moved to explore other approaches and further develop his ability to meaningfully bring God's word to such painful times.

THE DEATH OF A PERSON
WITH A HANDICAP

A person who has had a handicap throughout life faces problems and emotions that most of us do not begin to understand. I think of a friend whose difficult birth left her without the gift of sight, a gift that most of us take for granted. Another friend occasionally must take a leave-of-absence from work when her multiple sclerosis flares up, causing her hands and feet to turn at angles that make them non-functional. Still another friend contracted polio in the years before the Salk vaccine was developed. He survived the disease but spent his remaining life in a wheelchair.

All these persons might have become withdrawn and angry, bitter at God or life, but they did not. The woman without sight was one of the best organists with whom I have had the pleasure of working. The woman with multiple sclerosis regularly returns to her occupation of comforting and counseling anxious persons facing surgery. The polio victim, one of my most deeply committed lay leaders, regularly gave of himself and his resources to develop caring ministries in our community.

The death of someone whose life has been marked by a struggle with a handicap raises issues of God's power and love. Parents wonder what possible reason God might have for not giving them a child with all her faculties. They may wonder why God seems not to respond to their prayers for healing their child. They are not the first to experience such perplexity. Paul wrote "Three times I besought the Lord" about his own physical problem without the result for which he prayed (II Cor. 12:8).

When a child with a handicap dies, parents frequently link their search for the meaning of their child's life to its brevity. Because life was so short, parents may judge it meaningless; but, as one clergy-person noted, "One can give praise for life as God's gift even when the life of a child is ended prematurely, as was our daughter's. The three years of her life were a gift which her death cannot erase."[3]

The death of persons with handicaps, particularly children, makes many wonder why, given the amount of money and research that has been devoted to the disease, a cure cannot be discovered. The national offices of the organizations devoted to finding cures for handicaps can provide the clergy person with material that can assist her in understanding the illnesses. Books such as Leo Buscaglia's *The Disabled and Their Parents*,[4] or Charlotte E. Thompson's *Raising a Handicapped Child*[5] can help the pastor enter the world of handicapping conditions and understand the obstacles faced by persons with handicaps and their families.

A number of texts might be used to form the thrust of the sermon. The sermon may urge us to channel our grief into the struggle against a handicap and to perceive that struggle as a way in which we may take part in God's call to us to conquer and subdue the earth (Gen. 1:28).

In II Corinthians 4:7, Paul wrote of how we can be instruments of God who works through our weakness. The verses that follow illustrate the way in which persons may triumph in spite of their pain. Church bookstores contain many books written by persons whose courage and determination has helped them lead meaningful lives in spite of their handicaps. As Paul wrote, though we are "earthen vessels," and may feel "afflicted in every way," we are "not crushed" (4:7, 8).

Second Corinthians 12:8 reminds us that, though our prayers for wholeness may not receive the answer that we seek, there is power to be found in weakness. Verse 10 illustrates Paul's ability to accept the life that he was given and to learn "to be content with weakness."

First Corinthians 1:27 points out that "God chose what is foolish in the world to shame the wise, God chose what is weak in the world to shame the strong . . ." People with handicaps remind us, through their own strength, of physical abilities that we possess undeveloped. While escorting my organist to the church one afternoon, she reminded me of how well she was able to live without her eyesight. I tried to alert her to an entrance pillar that we were approaching. She was already aware of it, having noted the change in the force of the afternoon breeze on her face.

First Corinthians 15:42-43 illustrates how the Resurrection transforms the weak and perishable into a form "raised in glory" and "power." Though we are weak, imperfect, and "of the dust" (15:48), God makes of us a new creation in which we "bear the image of the man of heaven" (15:49).

The following sermon takes Matthew 25:21 as a text: "Well done, good and faithful servant . . . enter into the joy of your master." The text is part of Jesus' parable of the talents. Two of the servants in the parable brought a return on the money entrusted to them by their master; one of them did nothing with the money left with him. All of us are not born with equal amounts of talent or ability. God does not expect a return on that which we do not possess, but God does expect us to do the best we can with the life that has been given to us. A popular television commercial tells us that "A mind is a terrible thing to waste." We are not given abilities so that we may place them on display unused, dusting them off for viewing whenever visitors come. Even those with severe handicaps can make the most of the life that God has given to them. The following sermon speaks of one such man. Having lived his entire life with severe diabetes, he nevertheless overcame all of the effects of the disease, used his ability to establish a successful business, and freely gave of his resources to help others.

THE SERMON

Text: "Well done, good and faithful servant . . . enter into the joy of your master." *(Matt. 25:21)*

Ordinarily, I approach a sermon for a service like this with a great deal of anxiety. "What in the world," I wonder, "can I say to people who have lost someone at the age of 43?"

My first reaction was one of anger when I heard the news. When the hospital called to tell me that _____ had died of a massive heart attack, it seemed so unfair to me that I couldn't even begin to think about what I might say until my own angry feelings had eased. His heart attack seemed the final insult to a life marked by illness. Yet, through it all, he had the time to become my friend. Because of that, what I am going to say about him today will be very personal.

You all knew _____. He contracted diabetes very early in his life. Because of that disease, he lost his eyesight at a young age. Perhaps he despaired, but not for long. He went to a school for sightless people and learned to get along without his eyes.

You all knew _____. He was the man who, little by little, lost bits and pieces of his legs to diabetes until he completely lost both legs. He may have despaired, but not for long. He learned to get along without them.

You all knew _____. He was a man who did not always live in such a way that everyone agreed with him. He was no saint; you know that. But then neither are you or I. Most of us probably would not get along very well with saints, anyway. No, praise God, _____ was not a saint. He took his pleasure in little ways as he could find it. In his condition, who could blame him? He lived his life as he wanted to, day by day.

You all knew _____. He never beat around the bush. He told you straight out what he was thinking. He had a pretty clear sense of his own identity. You never had to try to figure him out; what you saw was what you got with _____. And that was the way he accepted others also.

However, when he was straightforward, he always had a sense of humor. He might say to me, "Gee that was a terrible sermon today!" And I could respond with, "Well, if you don't like it here, you know you can always go somewhere else!" Then both of us would laugh. But, I'm not telling you anything you do not already know, because you knew _____.

If anyone ever wrestled with God's plan for him, if anyone ever struggled to understand why life for him was what it was, it was _____. Yet, never did you hear a murmur of complaint from him. He learned to take life with "no thought for the morrow." But, again, you know all of that.

I'd like to tell you about the _____ that you did not know. You would not have known because he was always careful to keep it to himself. Only a few of us knew. Because he is not here to "fight" with me I am going to take the liberty to tell you more about him.

I want to tell you about the _____ who loved our young people. It wasn't only to promote trade that the shelves at the entrance to _____'s store were full of toys. He wanted the children to pick them up and play with them while their parents shopped.

I want to tell you about the _____ who, on several occasions, donated $1,000 to the church and ear-marked it for youth work. We have the equipment for a new confirmation program this year because _____ was interested in it. We have a large group of junior-high youth going to a conference-wide retreat at Green Lake because _____ provided money to pay for the transportation. You did not know about it, because that was the way he wanted it. The donations were always made anonymously.

I want to tell you about the _____ who always came to church: first, because he wanted to, and second, because of the generosity of the friend who brought him. I want to tell you about the _____ who always attended our adult Sunday school class. He did not just come; he came prepared. His friend had already read the lesson to him. Some of you will remember the time he arrived late for class and entered with that grin on his face. Why was he late? Because he was sitting out in the parking lot boning up on the lesson!

I want you to know about the _____ who came to all sorts of special occasions at the church. Take our church picnic, for example. I suspect that he came primarily because I bragged about my ability to play horseshoes. He sat at the court, waiting for me to play, so that he could give me the "raspberry" when, as usual, my mouth proved to be bigger than my ability. That was the _____ that some of us knew. There was no pretension to him. He did what he did quietly, as Jesus suggested, never letting his left hand know what the right was doing.

When I began writing about him, I remembered an experience I read in Merle Miller's biography of President Harry S Truman. After Truman left the White House and returned to his home in Independence, Missouri, he was interviewed by a reporter who wanted to know what was the first thing he did on his first night back in civilian life. Expecting a profound answer, the reporter was disappointed when Truman responded with, "Well, I carried the (suit-cases) up to the attic."[6] _____ was like that. He was quiet, dedicated, deeply loyal; he gave more of himself than anyone ever knew.

So, I ask you, can we be sad at his passing? If funerals are supposed to be mournful affairs, this one is just not going to cut the mustard. In spite of all the tremendous handicaps that _____ faced, he conquered them, and when such as he go to meet the Lord, we can not mourn that meeting. He was one of God's "salty" Christians who did not have to parade his piety for everyone to see. He simply lived quietly the way he felt Christ said we should. To those who do that, God has but one thing to say: "Well done, good and faithful servant; . . . enter into the joy of your Master." I cherish that gift for him.

Notes

1. *Preaching at Funerals*, Grove Booklets on Ministry and Worship (Bramcote Notts), p. 6.

2. "Thoughts on My Wife's Death," in *But Not to Lose: A Book of Comfort for Those Bereaved*, ed. Austin K. Kutscher (New York: Frederick Fell, 1969), p. 41.
3. Bruce C. Birch, "Biblical Faith and the Loss of Children," *The Christian Century* (Oct. 26, 1983): p. 967.
4. (New York: Holt, Rinehart, and Winston, 1983).
5. (New York: Ballantine, 1987).
6. *Plain Speaking: An Oral Biography of Harry S Truman* (New York: Berkley Publishing Group, 1974), p. 17.

DEATH BY SUICIDE

Death by suicide raises so many issues that it is one of the most difficult of funerals to prepare. Though there are instances of suicide in the Bible—Ahithophel (II Sam. 17:23), Saul (II Sam. 1:5-10), Samson (Judg. 16:28-31), Judas (Matt. 27:1-5)—the Bible makes no judgment upon the morality of the act. The same cannot be said of persons. In some quarters of Christendom for example, suicide is regarded as a sin of such magnitude as to rule out the decedent's entrance into heaven.[1]

The issue is not so clear-cut, especially when one considers contemporary medical and legal practice. It is common for patients with a terminal illness, for example, to instruct their physicians not to resuscitate them in the event of a cardiac arrest. Living wills request medical staff to refrain from the use of heroic life-sustaining measures or equipment. Issues of euthanasia and a patient's right to die with dignity are very much a matter of discussion in medical bio-ethical circles. When "the degree of suffering reaches the point that the disintegration of human personality begins, or when it is certain that the natural course of events will lead to imbecility or a vegetable existence, then a decision to terminate life might not be incongruent with proper self-love and servanthood."[2] The principle matter for consideration is quality of life, *not* the morality of allowing persons to die.

There are psychological issues that are uniquely present in suicide survivors as well. Although they experience all of the manifestations of grief common to most bereaved persons, suicide survivors may feel an additional measure of guilt. They may feel that they should have been able to work out the problems that led to the suicidal act. They may feel guilt at not perceiving the so-called warning signs indicating that the deceased was considering such an act. Thus, "the suicidal person places his psychological skeleton in the survivor's closet."[3] Family members feel stigmatized by the act.

Numerous volumes are available that provide more information to the pastor.[4] Of particular value to me is Edwin Schneidman's *Definition of Suicide.* Schneidman's examination of the common stressors, goals, and emotions found in many suicides is very helpful to those seeking to understand how someone could take his own life.[5] For families whose lives have been shattered by the suicide of one of their children, the Centering Corporation offers a helpful booklet, *Suicide of a Child.*[6]

Families feeling a sense of shame may try to keep a suicide secret. This can create an awkward situation at the funeral in which the unspoken "secret" not only interferes with the congregation's ability to hear the sermon's word of hope, but also prevents friends from really being "present" to the bereaved family with the support that they need.

If sensitively mentioned at the beginning of the sermon, the entire question can be removed from consideration, leaving the way clear to focus upon

God's word of solace to those who mourn. If the question of judgment looms large in the congregation, Matthew 7:1-5 speaks to our human tendency to condemn, reminding us that "with the judgment you pronounce you will be judged, and the measure you give will be the measure you get."

Psalm 139 speaks of the God who has searched us and known us, in spite of what we do or where we go. Indeed, even when we would hide in darkness, we discover that "darkness is as light with God" (139:12).

The Bible's message is one of grace. It tells us that God accepts us as we are. We cannot "change" ourselves to somehow become worthy of God's grace. John 3:16 tells us that "whoever believes in him should not perish but have eternal life." It does not say anything about the manner of our dying. In fact, it specifically states that God sent Jesus "not to condemn the world, but that the world might be saved through him" (3:17).

When the deceased is a young person, as is often the case today, parental concern for the welfare of the child is a strong dynamic.[7] The Good Shepherd passages in John 10 speak of the shepherd's love for his sheep (10:10-17, 27-30).

For those who may wonder whether the deceased will get into heaven, the Bible's silence on the matter ought to be sufficient. In addition, Romans 8:1 tells us that for those who are in Christ Jesus "there is therefore now no condemnation." Nothing, other than a strong proclamation of God's love for all of us, made real in Jesus' Resurrection, needs to be said.

When I began to prepare the sermon that follows, I had a deep awareness of the "burden" of pain carried by the decedent. Revelation 21:4 seemed to speak to that pain with God's promise to "wipe away every tear" in a place where there was no longer any "mourning nor crying nor pain." This verse from the Apocalypse carries with it echoes of the Exile and Israel's desire to return to its own beloved kingdom. Isaiah promised that the "voice of weeping shall no more be heard" in God's city (65:19).

The sermon begins by confronting the question of suicide's morality and illustrates the dilemma through the deaths of Henry Pitney Van Dusen and his wife. William Stringfellow saw their death as "the only way" for the Van Dusens "to value their own humanity in life" by dying "humanly by their own decision and act, instead of as victims of radical disability . . ."[8] Stringfellow felt that their death recalled the first century deaths of the Israelites on Masada.

Isaiah wrote that in God's kingdom God "will wipe away tears from off all faces" (25:8). If Revelation was written during a time of intense persecution of the early Christians, those suffering believers knew more than their share of pain and sadness. The suicide of someone we love brings a hurt that can be approached only by the belief that, in God's presence, "the former things have passed away" (Rev. 21:4).

THE SERMON

Text: "He will wipe away every tear from their eyes, and death shall be no more, neither shall there be mourning nor crying nor pain any more, for the former things have passed away." *(Rev. 21:4)*

Several years ago, Henry Pitney Van Dusen, internationally famous scholar, author, and former president of New York's prestigious Union Theological Seminary, and his wife took an overdose of sleeping pills and ended their lives. Although they left a letter explaining why they felt the need to commit suicide, the shock caused by their death reverberated throughout the theological world. Realizing that they were aging, the Van Dusens did not want to spend their remaining years in a nursing home, becoming a burden to anyone who might have to care for them. None of their reasons, however, lessened the amazement felt by many.

There were those who said that it was a terrible thing to do, that it was morally wrong. But there were others who, although they felt bad about the deaths, seemed to understand why the Van Dusens decided to act as they did.

One thing was very clear to me. It is not our responsibility to judge, in one way or another, the rightness or wrongness of their act. There is not one of us who is so wise as to completely understand the motives of another person.

On this side of the vale, we will never understand

what led _____ to do what she did, but it is not our responsibility to judge her.

Saying that, however, does not change the fact that she is gone. The manner of her passing leaves us with nothing but unanswered questions and feelings of intense frustration, especially when considering all that _____ had going for her.

_____ was a sensitive woman, a teacher who deeply felt the emotions of the students she had dedicated herself to educate. Blessed with a good mind, she had prepared herself well for what she wanted to do. When you think about how hard it seems to find teachers who care deeply about students, her death is especially sad.

_____ was a naturally outgoing people-person who related easily to others. Always willing to help others with their problems, always thinking of her family's needs, always faithfully remembering birthdays, always home for the holidays—she was always "there" for those who loved her. Her absence leaves an aching void in the life of her family. She gave so much of herself to others, but she also took their problems upon her own shoulders. When her students were hurt, she hurt.

Anyone who works in a helping profession will tell you that we just can't do what _____ tried to do. We are not strong enough to live other people's lives for them. When we take so much of their hurt into ourselves, it piles up until we bend or break under the load. I know of only one who was able to do that, and he did it so well that they led Jesus out of town, hung him on a cross, and watched him die.

I believe that just as Jesus took upon himself all of the frustration, hurt, and despair of his own time, he continues to do that for us. I believe that he has taken up _____'s struggle in his death, that he knows her better than any of us ever could, and that he holds her life in his hands.

I believe that the only way to cope with the pain we feel today is to rest upon the faith we have in the God who holds our lives in the grip of his love, no matter how far we stray.

He is not a God who sits far off, isolated and aloof from our pain. He is not a rock off of which our prayers rebound to us unanswered. He is one who knows our pain because he watched his own Son die. But, he is even more than that because he gave us a promise. He has prepared for us a "city," a city that does not know the tears, suffering, and frustration of this life. The New Testament describes it this way:

> And I saw the holy city . . . prepared as a bride adorned for her husband . . . and God himself will be with them; he will wipe away every tear from their eyes, and death shall be no more, neither shall there be mourning nor crying nor pain any more, for the former things have passed away. (Rev. 21:2-4)

In the midst of our despair, our questions, and our hurt, there is only one direction in which we can proceed. Just as _____ went to meet the Lord, we must put our trust in him to care for her in all the ways we wish we could. Only he is able to hold the hurt without breaking and to give us a new life in which "death shall be no more."

Notes

1. Howard W. Stone, *Suicide and Grief* (Philadelphia: Fortress, 1972), p. 60.
2. Terence R. Anderson, "Suicide and Moral Responsibility," in Richard N. Soulen, ed., *Care for the Dying* (Atlanta: John Knox, 1975), p. 34.
3. Edwin S. Schneidman, "To the Bereaved of a Suicide," in Austin H. Kutscher, ed., *But Not to Lose: A Book of Comfort for Those Bereaved* (New York: Frederick Fell, 1969), p. 60.
4. See John H. Hewett, *After Suicide* (Philadelphia: Westminster, 1980), or Mary Griffin, M.D., and Carol Felsenthal, *A Cry for Help* (Garden City, N.Y.: Doubleday, 1983).
5. (New York: John Wiley & Sons, 1985). See particularly pp. 121-52.
6. The Centering Corporation publishes a wide variety of helpful booklets relating to fetal, infant, and child death. A catalog of their publications is available at: The Centering Corporation, P.O. Box 3367, Omaha, NE 68103-0367.
7. A very moving account of the impact of a teenager's suicide on a clergy family was written by Corinne Chilstrom, "Suicide and Pastoral Care," in *The Journal of Pastoral Care*, vol. XLIII, no. 3 (Fall 1989): pp. 199-208.
8. *A Simplicity of Faith*, Journeys of Faith Series, Robert A. Raines, ed. (Nashville: Abingdon, 1982), p. 43.

A STRANGER TO
THE CHURCH

There are many communities where one church and its pastor conduct the majority of funerals involving persons who either did not attend church or were believed not to have followed the Bible's teachings about Jesus Christ. I believe that all persons have the right to a respectful funeral, and that it is not my responsibility to assume God's role of judging who is or is not acceptable to him. Each service represents an opportunity to reach out in ministry to persons not otherwise found in our congregations. If the service is sensitively done, it is not unusual for members of the deceased's family to initiate a relationship with the church. The pastor can find assistance in conducting these kinds of services in such manuals as Perry H. Biddle's *The Abingdon Funeral Manual*[1] or Robert Hughes' *A Trumpet in Darkness: Preaching to Mourners.*[2]

Among the psychological dynamics present in services for the unchurched, there may be guilt on the part of some family members who feel that they should have been able to bring the deceased into faith. This guilt may be exacerbated in those who, having grown up in the church's teachings, wonder if the deceased's lack of faith will prevent her from being accepted by God. Such guilt may lead families to spend large amounts of money on the funeral or to make a large contribution to the church in the hope that God will be influenced by their generosity. The issue of judgment must be addressed. Two biblical passages speak directly to this issue. In John 10:16, Jesus specifically told his disciples that there were "other sheep," not of their group, who were loved nonetheless. Matthew 7:1 contains Jesus' specific admonition against judging other persons. W. A. Poovey said it well: "The preacher is not the judge of the dead and he is not called on to wound the living. Even a scoundrel may have some people who mourn his passing."[3]

The story of the thief on the cross (Luke 23:39-43) offers preaching possibilities, particularly for those persons who brought to their death a measure of faith.

I have known many persons who never affiliated with the church but whose lives could have served as examples for any Christian. Matthew 25:31-46 focuses our attention on people whose deep caring caused them to hear Jesus' word of approval (vs. 34). We can have faith that God knows who we are, even if other people do not (Ps. 139:1-6).

The following sermon is based upon Jesus' story of the pharisee and the publican (Luke 18:9-14). Jesus set the story in the Jerusalem temple area. In the midst of the crowd coming to worship, two men stood out. One of them, the pharisee, held himself aloof from the other people lest he be contaminated by their sin. He knew himself to be righteous and reminded God not only of the vices from which he abstained, but also of all of his deeds above and beyond what was required of him.

The publican, or tax collector, also knew who he was and humbly prayed for forgiveness from his sin. He stood out on the fringe of the crowd as well, but, unlike the pharisee, the publican did not feel worthy enough to draw nearer to the temple.

Both men knew who they were and told the truth about themselves to God. One was pompous; the other was humble. There are many people in our congregations whose piety resembles that of either the pharisee or the publican. The man for whom I wrote this sermon was like the publican. He knew who he was and did not pretend to be any more than that. He never attended church, but he was generous with his time and his resources when they could help others. W. H. Auden wrote, "We who must die demand a miracle."[4] The miracle has been given; it is summarized in Jesus' verdict on the publican. "I tell you, this man went down to his house justified" (Luke 18:14a).

THE SERMON

Text: "Every one who exalts himself will be humbled, but he who humbles himself will be exalted." *(Luke 18:14b)*

Those of us who give part of our lives in service to the church sometimes assume that the church is the place for a Christian to be found. Now and then, we even can become impressed with our own goodness.

When that happens, I'm reminded of the pharisee who was criticized by Jesus for reminding God of all of his charitable acts, and for thanking God that he was not as bad as the tax collector who he could see out on the edge of the crowd. The church has its share of pharisees.

We gather here tonight in memory of a man who was more like the tax collector, or publican, than the pharisee. _____ was not a man who came to church often. Whether or not that was good is not our concern, however, for _____ was a genuinely good man. That is the bottom line. That makes his sudden death hard on those who knew and loved him the most.

I'm not going to spend a great deal of time telling you what he was like. It was not like _____ to talk about himself. The service will not be lengthy, either. _____'s family has asked that we be brief, and _____ would not have wanted a long, drawn-out affair. He was simple and straightforward, with very little shame or hypocrisy, rather like the publican, who did not try to persuade God that he was something that both he and God knew he was not. He said it very simply: "God, be merciful to me, a sinner." That said all that needed to be said, and when you come right down to it, that's really all that any of us can say at any given time in our lives. I think _____ knew that.

In many ways, _____ reminded me of someone that I knew at a previous parish. I tried and tried to persuade that fellow to come to church, but all of the standing and sitting, and closing and opening of the eyes just was not his cup of tea. But, the more I came to know him, I discovered that under his gruff surface there lived a man with a deep concern for people. I can't remember the number of times I took to him persons who were in one kind of trouble or another, knowing that he would help them get their lives back on track. For a person who never attended church, he had a remarkably Christ-like ability to feel with and for persons who hurt. He thoroughly helped disabuse me of the notion that the greatest persons in the world were those who were sitting in front of a pulpit every Sunday morning.

The death of people such as _____ leaves us poorer. Not that we did not expect _____'s death. We did. There was an inevitability about his illness and, no doubt, his death saved him from further suffering—something for which we can, perhaps, be grateful.

Knowing that, however, does not change the feelings that remain: the sadness, the loneliness, the hurt, and the subtle reminder of our own mortality. These feelings are left for us to deal with; yet, are these feelings not made easier to handle by the knowledge that someone has been there before us? At seventy-five years of age, _____ has gone to a reward of which we are but dimly aware. We know it only through the Lord who said, "I go to prepare a place for you." Standing as we are on the brink of Easter, we are reminded by this verse that God keeps his promises.

The church stands today as a constant reminder that God's goodness and love extend beyond our

imagining and well past our poor grasp of time. Were
our salvation to have rested upon human faithfulness, we would have been lost long ago. We are not
lost, and even as we give _____ over to the
arms of the One who gave him to us, we do so with a
sense of gratitude to God who gives us life abundant.

Notes

1. (Nashville: Abingdon, 1984).
2. (Philadelphia: Fortress, 1985). See also Mark Coppenger,
   "Funerals for Those You Barely Know," in *Leadership*,
   Spring, 1987.
3. *Planning a Christian Funeral* (Minneapolis: Augsburg,
   1978), p. 38.
4. "For the Time Being," *The Collected Poetry of W. H.
   Auden* (New York: Random House, 1945), p. 411.

THE DEATH
OF A CHILD

There are very few experiences with death that equal the pain felt at the death of a child. Not only must the parents struggle with the intense anguish that they feel, but pastor and congregation also find themselves confronting one of their worst fears. We expect our children to out-live us. When they do not, the entire creation seems out of kilter.

In order to understand the dynamics that are a part of this experience of death, we need to distinguish several ways that a child's death may be experienced. Parental feelings seem to focus at different points, for example, if death is the result of stillbirth rather than Sudden Infant Death Syndrome (SIDS). One of the most helpful sources for acquiring further information about each of these forms of infant death is the Centering Corporation; their booklets are widely used by caregivers.[1]

The church has not given enough attention to prenatal death (more commonly referred to as "spontaneous abortion" or "miscarriage"). The death of a fetus causes intense grieving in many parents. Occasionally, the pastor may be called upon to conduct a brief service for the interring of the remains.[2] Spontaneous abortion confronts the parents with the fear that they may not be able to produce a healthy child. The feelings of anger and injustice that are a part of almost all child-death experiences are present here as well. There is a feeling of bitterness that the unborn child was never given an opportunity to experience life. Parents, particularly if unwed may feel guilty, believing that they failed to do something that might have prevented the death.

Stillbirth is the experience of having completed a long and sometimes difficult process of nurturing the life and growth of a child only to be denied the reward at birth. When it is known a few weeks in advance that the child has died "in utero," as is often the case, the mother may have to carry the child to term and experience a normal process of labor, all the while feeling that her love and labor are wasted. The mother may experience a loss of self-esteem, feel inadequate as a female, and wonder why she cannot do what other mothers seem to do with ease. Pat Schwiebert's and Paul Kirk's book *Still to Be Born* is helpful to the pastor who would better understand this experience.[3]

SIDS deaths bring intense feelings of guilt to the parents. Having successfully passed through the process of fetal development and childbirth, parents may feel that the most anxious period is behind them. The sudden death of their child—with absolutely no warning, as is common with SIDS— leaves them feeling that they somehow should have known that it was coming and should have taken steps to prevent it. These feelings may be aggravated by misunderstanding on the part of other persons involved. Noting the absence of any immediately identifiable cause of death, investigative personnel

may suspect the parents of abuse or neglect. Parents
may wonder if their baby suffered. They need to be
informed that

> SIDS death can occur within five minutes and is
> almost instantaneous. It is assumed that there is
> some movement that occurs during the last few
> seconds, which would explain the rumpled blankets
> or unusual positions of the infant. SIDS infants do
> not cry out, neither do they show any trace of having
> been disturbed in their sleep. Authorities conclude
> from their investigations that SIDS does not cause
> suffering or pain to the baby.[4]

With the death of an older child, the psychodynamics are shifted once again. When parents lose a
son or daughter, not only do they experience the
death of a child, but they also confront the loss of part
of their legacy. In the hospital where I am employed,
there is a sign that reads: "Children are God's
assurance of the future." When children die, part of
our future, our legacy, dies with them.

The desire to protect our children from harm
represents what is probably one of the most basic of
parental instincts. A child's death reminds parents
"of the limit of their power: there is no time in life
when they have greater motivation to act and yet are
helpless; they cannot protect a defenseless child."[5]

The feeling of powerlessness varies according to
circumstances. It is greatest when a child's death is
the result of a sudden accident. On the other hand,
when a child dies as a result of a long terminal illness
during which the parents have been enabled to care

for the child, the powerlessness may be lessened by the belief that "we did all that we could for her." The ability to express their love can be a tremendously important factor in helping parents to heal. One bereaved mother wrote, "Our feelings were mostly of relief that (our daughter) was finally at peace. We felt privileged to have been her parents, for she had taught us so much."[6]

When a child dies, one of the most significant theological issues facing the pastor has to do with the meaning of the child's life. When life is cut off well before the child has a chance to fully experience the world around it or to make a contribution, the life seems to be almost meaningless. "Why was he born if he was going to live only such a short time?" parents may ask.

Issues of God's love and power are often present and expressed in questions such as, "Why did God not protect her? Doesn't God love children?" Common also are questions about the efficacy of prayer. Care must be taken not to make it appear that God took the child. Expressions such as "God wanted him" can make God appear to be a sadistic being who has little regard for our needs. "It's God's will" may cause parents to respond, "If that's God's will, then I want nothing to do with him." In *Preaching to Sufferers: God and the Problem of Pain,* I have discussed these issues in depth and have developed a theological approach that has been helpful in ministry to families touched by infant death.[7] In preparing to preach in this context, it is important to identify the meaning in the child's life, regardless of its length. It has been said that

> suffering ceases to be suffering when it has meaning, and I feel that this is what happened inside me when I first heard that (our daughter) would not be with us for long. I saw her as a teacher, as I saw all those terminal children. They were all exceptional human beings, and their lives did have meaning. We are constantly reminded of the lessons that she taught us.[8]

There are many scriptural passages from which texts may be taken for preaching. Any of the shepherd passages that express God's care for his sheep (Isa. 40:11, John 10:10ff) serve to reassure us that "he will gather the lambs in his arms." Mark 13 tells of how Jesus took the children "in his arms and blessed them." Those who have cared for a child have cared for Jesus himself (Mark 9:37).

Not only does Jesus have a special love for children, but childlikeness and innocence may be seen as marks of those who would enter the kingdom of heaven (Matt. 18:1-4). The story of the raising of the son of the widow at Nain may be seen as a paradigm of the new life given to our children after death. In using this story, however, care must be taken to avoid leading the bereaved parents to wonder why God seemed to not respond to their prayers for healing for their child. John Updike saw the issue: "It is . . . not upon the plausibility of . . . miracles but upon their selectivity that we stumble."[9]

The sermon that follows was delivered at the funeral for a one-year-old boy who came home from the hospital for only a short time after birth. He became ill and spent the remaining months of his life in the hospital's neo-natal intensive care unit. Those months were a roller-coaster of joy and pain for his parents as they watched him rally one day and then decline the next. The hospital staff became quite attached to him, as frequently happens with long-term patients. On the evening when he died, his room was filled with tearful hospital staff, in addition to his parents. Many of them attended his funeral.

The text for the sermon is Matthew 9:14: "Let the children come to me, and do not hinder them; for to such belongs the kingdom of God." Well-known public figures frequently have body-guards to protect them from the crowds that press around them. Perhaps that was the role that Jesus' disciples sought to play when they discouraged people from bringing their children to Jesus for a blessing. Jesus rebuked them and taught them a lesson about the characteristics of those who would enter the kingdom of heaven. Childlikeness, innocence, trust, and a dependence upon God's grace are the marks of those who would come to Jesus. Those marks are still best seen in children.

As I read the story of Jesus and the children, I thought of children's sermons that I have done. They can be only partially prepared in advanced. The finished product depends upon the very honest and engaging remarks made by the children, remarks that teach us much about a child's view of life, a view too soon forgotten in our rush to become adults.

In coming to Jesus, children return to their origin. George Buttrick reminds us that "Our children are not our children, for we can only transmit life: we cannot create life."[10]

THE SERMON

Text: "Let the children come to me, and do not hinder them; for to such belongs the kingdom of heaven." *(Matt. 19:14)*

In pediatric units in hospitals all over the nation you might see paintings similar to the one that hangs in our hospital. It is a portrait of Jesus kneeling among a group of children, holding out his arms to hug them. The painting is a modern retelling of the gospel story about the parents who brought their children to Jesus to receive a blessing. The disciples, perhaps feeling that Jesus was too busy with more important matters, tried to shoo the children away. But Jesus rebuked them saying, "Let the children come to me . . . for to such belongs the kingdom of heaven."

I wonder where we would be today if someone had decided that this story was not important enough to be included in the Gospels. After all, Jesus did not spend a great deal of time with children. The stories that we have, however, make it clear that Jesus had a special love for children.

There are many gathered here who share this special love. We are here because this love has been fractured. After giving all that we knew to give for a year, and after doing everything we knew to help him, _____ died last Tuesday night.

_____ spent most of his life in the hospital. Those of you who cared for him in the Neo-Natal Intensive Care Unit came to know him very well. In the months that he was your guest, you nursed him over one crisis after another. His condition improved and we became hopeful; then it worsened again and we worried. He kept us hopping.

The other thing that he did, by virtue of being in the unit for so long, was to worm his way into our affections and take up residence there. We watched him grow, become pudgy, start cutting teeth, and all of the other things that babies do as they begin to develop personalities of their own.

Three times a week or more, as I made my rounds, I visited _____ and was amazed at the way he hung on through everything that threatened to knock the props out from under him. That this did not happen is a tribute to the care given by the medical and nursing staff and to _____'s own tenacity. _____ was one tough little boy.

Even so, tough or not, he is gone. No one is more aware of that than his parents. _____ and _____. You have had that special love, the love that said "Let the children come to me"; let

_____ get well; let him come home. You did everything you could to make it happen.

"Let the children come to me. . . ." At first we almost want to respond by saying, "There's no way I'm going to let go of him." That's honest, for love holds closest what is dearest to us. Yet, when we are given no choice in the matter, it is at least good to know that we give him up to One whose love for him is just as special as ours. Jesus said "Let the children come to me" not to cause us pain, but to assure us that he would care for the children and give them all of the love that we wish we could give.

But what about us? What can we take from an experience like this? I think we take from it questions about the meaning of a life that was so short and was lived almost entirely in the hospital. Theologian Martin Marty said, "Sensitive people have to make sense of the . . .world."[11]

Where, then, can sensitive people find sense in _____'s short life? Many would say that the very shortness of his life robs it of meaning. I don't believe that. If long life is the basis of meaning, then Jesus' life does not mean much. Nor does Lincoln's or Kennedy's or King's. No, length has little to do with it.

Rabbi Harold Kushner, whose book *When Bad Things Happen to Good People* sprang out of the death of his son, wrote, "I am a more sensitive person, a more effective pastor, a more sympathetic counselor because of Aaron's life and death than I would ever have been without it."[12] I would confirm

that out of my own experience. _____'s life and
death has sensitized all of us to the feelings of people
who go through this. All of us who work daily in the
presence of love and death will do so better than
before because we've been touched by _____'s
life.

Henri Nouwen said it well: "Sorrow is an
unwelcome companion and . . . anyone who will-
ingly enters into the pain of a stranger is truly a
remarkable person."[13] _____'s death presented
us with the opportunity to minister in just that way.

You (parents) have had the same experience. You
will know it better when the pain of losing
_____ becomes more bearable. You will find
that you are more open to the feelings of others who
hurt, and therefore are better friends and more
compassionate parents.

We may say, "Thanks, but I'd rather have
_____." So would I, and so would an endless
line of parents whose children have died. So also
would the God of our faith who grieved the death of
his own Son, but gave to him the gift of renewed life.
And, in the end, it is that upon which we must rely.
Jesus said, "He who has seen me has seen the father"
(John 14:9). In Jesus' special love for children the
very nature of God himself is revealed. "Let the
children come to me" is God's promise to love them
for us until such time as we can love them again. "Let
the children come to me . . . for to such belongs the
kingdom of heaven." That is God's gift to _____
on his first birthday.

Notes

1. I have found the following booklets to be especially helpful:
   Newborn Death (miscarriage and stillbirth), 1982
   Why Mine? (the seriously ill child), 1981
   Miscarriage (fetal death), 1983
   No New Baby (for children whose expected sibling dies),
   1988
   These and a catalog of other available booklets can be
   ordered from: The Centering Corporation, P.O. Box 3367,
   Omaha, NE 68103-0367.
2. A helpful resource for pastors and parents is by Mary Beth
   Franklyn, *After Pregnancy Loss* (Available from: Disciple-
   ship Resources, P.O. Box 189, Nashville, TN 37202).
3. Pat Schwiebert, R.N., and Paul Kirk, M.D., *Still to Be
   Born*, 1986. Available from: Perinatal Loss, 2116 N.E.
   18th Avenue, Portland, Oregon 97212.
4. Polly Doyle, *Grief Counseling and Sudden Death*
   (Springfield, Ill.: Charles C. Thomas, 1980), p. 76.
5. Irvin Yalom, *Existential Psychotherapy* (New York: Basic
   Books, 1980), pp. 70-71.
6. Brenda Comerford, "Parental Anticipatory Grief and
   Guidelines for Caregivers," in Bernard Schoenberg et al.,
   Anticipatory Grief (New York: Columbia University Press,
   1974), p. 152.
7. (Nashville: Abingdon, 1988).
8. Comerford, "Parental Anticipatory Grief and Guidelines
   for Caregivers," p. 152.
9. *A Month of Sundays* (Greenwich, Conn.: Fawcett
   Publications, 1974), p. 124.
10. *God, Pain, and Evil* (Nashville: Abingdon, 1966), p. 74.
11. *A Cry of Absence: Reflections for the Winter of the Heart*
    (San Francisco: Harper & Row, 1983), p. 14.
12. (New York: Avon Books, 1983), pp. 133-34.
13. *In Memoriam* (Notre Dame, Ind.: Ave Maria Press, 1980),
    p. 14.

THE DEATH OF A
YOUNG PARENT FROM CANCER

This section combines two issues whose dynamics are frequently intertwined: cancer and the death of a young parent. When a young person dies, cancer is often the cause. The death of a young adult raises many of the same issues as the death of a child. The shortness of life seems unfair and without meaning. A sense of powerlessness in the face of death's inevitability may elicit anger. The anger may be directed at God. God may be perceived as having betrayed the trust given to him by the deceased.

When the young person is a parent as well, several additional psychodynamics may be present. Robbing children of a mother or father heightens the feeling of injustice. In such instances children are forced to face the reality of death before they are able to understand it. A unique experience of powerlessness is found in children who, accustomed to being protected by their parents, suddenly discover that there is at least one force in life against which their parents are powerless. If mother or father cannot escape death, then who will protect the children?

If grandparents have preceded the parent in death, children quickly pick up the progression, realizing that the last "barrier" between them and the grave is now gone. The children realize they are next in line, and this is a terribly sobering realization. Although death can come at any age, death particularly affects small children who have not yet had a chance to come to grips with death's part in life. Great sensitivity and patience is required to help children cope with the loss of a parent.

The responsibility for helping the children cope with the death falls most often on the surviving spouse. That responsibility could not come at a worse time, for the surviving spouse is involved in coping with her own feelings.

> "The loss of a spouse often evokes the issue of basic isolation; the loss of the significant other . . . increases one's awareness that, try as hard as we may to go through the world two by two, there is nonetheless a basic aloneness that we must bear."[1]

When cancer is the cause of death, family members may feel beaten down, worn out by the experience. Initially, when cancer is first diagnosed and after the disbelief and anger is managed, persons may experience a fierce determination to fight against the disease. The all-encompassing nature of this fight may leave children feeling neglected.

Surgery often follows the diagnosis, separating the parent and his children during convalescence. If radiation or chemo-therapy follows the surgery, as is very common today, children may then be witness to the uncomfortable side effects that these therapies can cause. If the treatment seems to be successful, then celebration reigns. If, however, the cancer returns, celebration turns to gloom. To journey with a loved one through a fight against cancer is to experience a roller-coaster of emotions. There will

be long periods of frequent trips to and from hospital
and clinic for confinement or therapy. Family
members and friends may experience ambivalent
feelings, wanting to do all that they can to help and
yet resenting the disruption of their routine and
feeling guilty about the resentment.

Because much ignorance still exists about cancer,
persons fearing contagion may no longer come to
visit. Those who do come may seem reluctant to
touch the patient, adding to a sense of loneliness and
isolation that can be felt by the family. As the cancer
progresses toward death, it may disfigure the
patient. When death finally comes, there may be a
sense of relief at the end of the struggle. One of the
best books I have found for understanding cancer's
effect upon a patient and her family is *Taking Time*. It
is available through the National Cancer Institute.[2]

One of the most prevalent emotions found in
cancer patients and their families is anger. Children
may feel anger at the parent who left them against
their wishes. Anger may be directed against the
medical profession that cannot seem to find a cure for
the disease. Anger may be aimed at friends who no
longer come to visit, or a physician who may
suddenly become unavailable to the family once a
terminal assessment has been made. Anger may be
focused upon God who seems oblivious to the
family's prayers, or at the pastor who is seen as God's
representative. Theodore Isaac Rubin explores this
emotion in a helpful way in *The Angry Book*.[3]
National organizations such as "Can Surmount" and

"Make Today Count" can provide peer support for patients and their families.

A funeral sermon delivered for a young victim of cancer must give voice to the questions, doubt, and anger that exist in the family. We must avoid the appearance of protecting God from anger or defending him from doubt. Out of our hurt we say that such a death is unfair. I believe that God shares this sense of unfairness. Jesus' death was unfair. But unfairness is not the point; there is no mileage to be found in it. The point is that God stands with us in our hurt, as vulnerable to pain as we are, and yet triumphs over that pain through new life given in Christ's resurrection. Indeed, it is only God who can give us a sense of having beaten the cancer that ground us down with its relentless inevitability. "Come to me," Jesus said to all who "labor and are heavy-laden, and I will give you rest" (Matt. 11:28).

A sermon text may emphasize the way in which a parent can be remembered. David's poignant instruction to Solomon at the time of his death reminds us of the need to walk in God's ways, "keeping his . . . commandments" (I Kings 2:2-3). Jesus spoke of how his Father could be seen in the things that he said and did (John 14:10-11). As children search for meaning in the death of their father, we can help them focus upon the ways that their father continues to be a part of their lives through his love and guidance.

Former Chicago Bear football player Gale Sayers wrote of his friendship with teammate Brian Piccolo, who was stricken with cancer. At Piccolo's funeral,

Sayers broke down in tears. Piccolo's wife, Joy, said
to Sayers:

> Don't be sorry, Gale . . . I'm happy now because I
> know Brian is happy, and I don't have to watch him
> suffer any more. He's through suffering now.
> She comforted me [Sayers thought] . . . if she
> can really be that composed, Brian must have really
> given her something. And I thought, Well, he gave
> us all something, all of us who were privileged to
> know him. And that helped compose me.[4]

Paul wrote of how faith can be passed on to her
children by a godly mother (II Tim. 1:5). The
best-known passage commemorating the role played
by a wife and mother is Proverbs 31:10-31. There are
many today, however, who would find this passage
descriptive of a way of life more characteristic of a
patriarchal society. Nevertheless, her children will
still "rise up and call her blessed" (vs. 31). Though
the vivid parental imagery speaks of God's work in
establishing the nation of Israel, "As one whom his
mother comforts, so [God] will comfort" us in our
pain (Isa. 66:13).

Cancer can cause great suffering. We may agonize
with someone who suffers, wishing all the while that
we might be able to relieve them of some of their
pain; however, just as "Weeping may tarry for the
night" we can be sure that "joy comes with the
morning" of God's kingdom (Ps. 30:5). Jesus sought
to prepare his disciples for his own death by helping
them and us to see that even though we "sorrow
now" Jesus will see us again and "hearts will rejoice"

with a joy that no one can take from us (John 16:22). Romans 8:18 speaks of Paul's conviction that the "sufferings of this present time are not worth comparing to the glory that is to be revealed to us." Jesus has promised us that through the Resurrection all of the hurt and fear that we have known will disappear.

The sermon that follows was preached at the funeral service for a young woman who died in her early thirties. She was a high-school teacher and cheerleading coach whose death impacted not only her husband and two young children, but also touched the lives of many high school faculty and students. Many of these persons were present at the service.

There were many issues to be addressed by the sermon. She underwent a great degree of suffering that heightened the sense of injustice. Henri Nouwen felt this at the death of his mother and asked:

> Why were we witnessing such pain and agony in a woman whose life had been one of goodness, gentleness, tenderness and love? . . . Often friends suggested that it was unfair. . . . But do we really understand? Slowly, as the long hours and days passed, I began to wonder if mother's struggle did not in fact reveal the awesome truth of God's love. Who was more loving than Jesus? Who suffered more than he. . . . Is it this agony that mother was called to share?"[5]

The text for the sermon, Hebrews 11:13, 16, is part of one of the great New Testament chapters on faith. The writer catalogs the names of the great biblical figures from the past, noting how they did not live long enough to see God's promises to them come true. In a sense, this is true of all of us. We never see or do all that we would. We are always wanderers, "strangers and exiles," on the earth, working our way like John Bunyan's Pilgrim toward the promised land. The woman for whom this sermon was written had a very supportive faith that helped her pass through the pain and death. Though the shortness of her life made it seem that she did not "receive what was promised," God "prepared for [her] a city."

THE SERMON

Text: "These all died in faith, not having received what was promised. . . . God is not ashamed to be called their God, for he has prepared for them a city." (Heb. 11:13, 16)

Among all of the values that we hold sacred, there is one called justice. Many of us find it hard to define justice, but it is something that we believe in deeply and are most aware of in its absence. If we do not receive justice when we feel that we should, we seldom lose any time letting others know that we are the victims of discrimination.

In any given disagreement between my two children, it is common to hear one of them say to the other, "That's not fair!" That is his way of saying, "It's not just."

A young mother who was keeping a vigil at the bedside of her gravely ill child said to me, "Why him?" That was her way of saying, "It's not just."

When two airplanes collide on a runway and hundreds are killed in the inferno, an entire world stares in horror at the television and says, "Lord, what a shame!" That is their way of saying, "It's not right; it's not just."

There is within each of us a sense of what is right and proper, and what is not. Lest we be prone to think that we are the only ones who have ever felt this way, let us remember there was a man who hung dying on a cross and who, out of the depths of his own pain, cried out, "My God, my God, why hast thou forsaken me?" (Mark 15:34). Though we may feel that no one understands our despair and our pain, there are times when the very heavens cry out at the injustice. Pain and suffering and death are timeless.

However, we must deal with the reality of *this* moment. We cannot tiptoe quietly around death, no matter how much we would like to avoid it. It is an unhappy and an unjust occasion that has brought us together. _____ has died. Words cannot begin to express the outrage that we feel at the death of someone so young, so vibrant, so happy, and so alive. Out of the pain in our hearts, we shake our fists at creation itself and ask "Why?"

Why someone so young? Why someone with so much to live for? Why a wife and mother with two little children? And when all of our anguished questions have been spent, there remains only what theologian Helmut Thielicke called "the silence of god." Jesus knew that. He also died young; he also shouted into the void, "My God, my God, why. . . ?"

If this is not quite enough to fuel our despair, then let us also consider that in the death of those whose lives are full of promise, we are reminded of our own mortality. If death can come to them, then what of us? There are forces within the creation that are evil, that are not just, that from time to time rise up, bringing pain and suffering and, yes, death, to us and to those whom we love.

We struggle against it with all that is within us. So did _____. She struggled to get to the awards banquet for her cheerleaders at the high school; she was unable to make it. "I'd like to live until Easter," she said; but she did not. She brushed off her cancer with great courage until the illness finally robbed her of even the strength to fight. All of us who were close to her found our lives uplifted by hers. Her courage was not lost upon us, nor will her love be forgotten.

There is a passage in the book of Hebrews that almost seems as if it was written for someone such as _____.

These all died in faith, not having received what was promised, but having seen it and greeted it from afar, and having acknowledged that they were strangers and exiles on the earth. For people who speak thus make it clear that they are seeking a homeland . . . They desire a better country, that is, a heavenly one. Therefore God is not ashamed to be called their God, for he has prepared for them a city. (11:13-14, 16)

There is the word of hope from the scripture if we can but hear it through the darkness of our hurt. The author of this passage spoke of the faithful people in the history of the church who died before Jesus was born, before Easter had come. This passage is based upon the life and death of One whose promise seemed to end before its fulfillment. Were his death to have been the end of God's love for us, we would not be gathered here today. We would be little more than exiles upon this tattered planet. There would be no purpose to life, no reason for being, no awareness that some things are right and others are not. We could not struggle against the injustice of life if God had not first endowed us with faith.

He who created us tells us that we must let go, that we must trust him to receive the life that he gave to _____. He whose death brought Easter into being accepted our pain within his own. In his Resurrection he made of us an Easter people who know that although life may at times be absurd and painful, there is purpose in our living and light in the darkness of our life's ending.

Not long ago I stood in the evening on the top of the world's tallest building and looked out over the city. Wherever I looked, I could see the crosses on the tops of churches marking the horizon. It is that way in cities all over the world. The cross towers over the darkness below. Here in our sanctuary that cross stands; but it is an empty cross, bearing no

image of death. He is not there; he is risen.
Wherever we go, he is there with us. So it is with
_____. "God is not ashamed to be called [her]
God, for he has prepared for [her] a city."

Notes

1. Irvin Yalom, *Existential Psychotherapy* (New York: Basic Books, 1980), p. 168.
2. National Institutes of Health publication no. 87-2059, 1986 reprint, available through: The National Institutes of Health, National Cancer Institute, Bethesda, Maryland 20892.
3. (New York: Collier's Books, 1969).
4. *I Am Third*, with Al Silverman and intro. by Bill Cosby (New York: Bantam, 1970), p. 81.
5. *In Memoriam* (Notre Dame, Ind.: Ave Maria Press, 1980).

THE DEATH
OF A FRIEND

One of the most difficult funerals a pastor may ever be called upon to conduct is that of a close personal friend. "If you do not know the family, it is hard to appreciate their grief. But if the deceased was well known to you and the mourners are close friends, that is even worse. Ministers feel that they dare not break down and weep at funerals."[1]

There have been many occasions on which I have felt myself struggling to hold my emotions in check for fear or being unable to complete the service. One such occasion was at a funeral conducted for the infant son of close friends soon after the death of my own son. The practice preaching was marked by tears that I could not hold back. Not only did I feel the parents' pain, but I felt my own uncompleted grief present in those tears.

Over the course of my ministry I have come to understand that the valiant struggle to keep one's feelings under control is not only futile but also is unnecessary. Our emotions are a natural part of who we are. To deny them is essentially to deny ourselves and to appear unreal or detached to those around us. Modern psychosocial writing contains many examples of the role played by the releasing and sharing of feelings. There have been many occasions when, gathered with a family at the bedside of someone recently deceased, I have felt my own tears beside crying family members. Universally, those family members have responded in the same manner as did the people around Jesus when he wept in front of Lazarus' tomb (John 11:36). The tears become a bond between pastor and family members; grief is shared at a deep level.

The following sermon was preached at the funeral of one of the most dedicated lay-men with whom it has ever been my privilege to minister. Over the years of our association we became close friends. He was in his 40's when stricken by the heart attack that took his life. Ironically, a week previous, he had undergone a physical examination and had been pronounced fit. There were many points in the sermon when I lost the struggle to control my emotions, especially as I related personal material. I finished the sermon in tears, tears that not only mourned his death but also celebrated God's gift of life to him. In his book *Friendship*, Martin Marty wrote that friendship is "born of emotions one does not quite understand, toward ends that one cannot at all foresee."[2]

I used John 14's promise of life as the text for the funeral sermon. I also might have used the powerful passage in which Jesus noted the change in relationship between himself and his disciples, a change from servanthood to friendship (John 15:14-15).

John 14:2 is one of the verses in which Jesus attempted to prepare his disciples for his coming death announced in 13:33. He explained it in terms of going on ahead and preparing the way for those who would follow him. In a very real way his friendship would be with them when they went through the times of persecution and death that lay ahead of them. A dying student-nurse said, "All I want to know is that there will be someone to hold my hand when I need it. I am afraid. Death may get to be a routine to you, but it is new to me."[3] A friend is a person who is present with support when you need it.

A friend is also someone who goes on ahead, preparing the way through difficult times. On a backpacking trip through a dense swampy area, I found the way prepared by a friend who had blazed the trail ahead of me. Jesus said, "I go to prepare a place for you."

THE SERMON

Text: "In my Father's house are many mansions: if it were not so, I would have told you. I go to prepare a place for you." (*John 14:2 KJV*)

How do you say "good-bye" to a friend? Friends are so hard to find that you hate to let them go. For me, _____ was a friend. It's hard for me to say "good-bye."

He was not a fair-weather friend who was in a relationship for good times and then disappeared when things got tough. _____ took the good with the bad.

He was not a friend who was interested in what he could get out of the friendship. _____ was the kind of person who would give you the shirt off of his back if you needed it.

And he was not a friend who stuck with you only as long as you did things his way. Though he had a definite element of stubbornness, _____ wasn't afraid to try something new or different. So, how do you say "good-bye" to such a friend?

He was a man who loved the out-of-doors. He introduced me to trout fishing, deer hunting, and snowmobiling. He helped this "city-slicker" discover a part of himself that has continued to grow ever since.

He was a man who, like many of us males, had his share of "little boy" in his personality. Sometimes during hunting season, he would sit fascinated in his blind, watching the deer play around him, whittling little wooden tools instead of hunting.

He had a sense of humor that let him poke fun at my "citified" ways. His commitment to the church made him one of its most faithful supporters during the time when I was privileged to be his pastor. Although he was a somewhat reluctant participant in our district lay-speakers school, he nevertheless completed the school and was certified. He went on to preach and to receive rave reviews from our congregation. I don't know if he ever became accustomed to the praise or, for that matter, to wondering what his old school teachers would say if they could see him in a pulpit! He even participated in a Good Friday chancel drama that sent worshipers home with tears in their eyes.

I like to tell people that I built the office in this church; but, in all fairness, I never would have finished it if _____ had not spent some time helping me. He even tore down my furring strips and put them up again, all the while lecturing me about the meaning of "16-inches on center." All of these things and more make me wonder how in the world you say "good-bye" to a friend like _____.

We are not the first persons to have this problem. On the way to Jerusalem, knowing what was going to happen to him, Jesus thought about his friends. In my mind's eye I can picture him struggling with the knowledge of his coming death and the need to prepare his disciples for it. "How can I possibly explain this to them so that they will understand it?" he might have wondered. "How will they handle the pain of my death? How in the world do I say good-bye to my friends?"

On the way to the brutal death that took him away from his disciples in his early thirties, with what seemed to be all of the promise of his life yet ahead of him, Jesus tried to say good-bye. "You know, I'm going to be leaving you" (John 7:33, paraphrase). But they did not seem to understand. He tried again. "Now you see me, but in a little while you won't" (John 16:16, paraphrase). They looked at him as if he were talking in riddles. Finally, he said it about as clearly as he could: "In my Father's house are many mansions . . . I go to prepare a place for you" (John 14:2, KJV).

There are two particularly important lessons to be learned from all of this. The first of them is that saying good-bye is hard. Our emotions are such that we don't handle this very well, especially when we must say good-bye to someone as young as _____. We feel a sense of injustice. The world seems out-of-joint, and it hurts.

Even so, we know that there are deaths like _____'s that come quickly, and there are those that are filled with pain and sadness, that seem to linger on and on. During the last days of his life, Supreme Court Justice John Harlan tried to continue to run his law practice from his hospital bed. Nearly blind, he could hardly see what he was doing, let alone read petitions to the Court. One day a court clerk brought him an emergency petition. After discussing it, they both agreed that it should be denied. Harlan bent over, with his eyes almost on the paper, and signed his name. He gave the paper to his clerk who couldn't find the signature on it. "Justice Harlan, you just denied your sheet," the clerk said as he pointed to the ink scrawl on the linen. So Harland tried again.[4] How sad when life becomes a constant struggle to do the simplest things. That was not the kind of life that _____ would have wanted.

It is the second lesson from Jesus' experience that speaks to me the most. The answer to the question "How do you say good-bye to a friend?" is simply that you cannot. I'm not even going to try to do it. I think that Jesus, realizing that his disciples would never understand him, said it in the only way that makes any sense at all: "I go to prepare a place for you, that where I am, there you may be also." It is not good-bye; it is nothing less than a reminder to us that there are no good-byes. That is the absolutely amazing gift that Jesus gave to us, and to _____: the simple yet mind-boggling conviction that there are no longer good-byes. There are only "see you in the morning's." We thank God for that, even as we now give _____ over to that dawn.

Notes

1. W. A. Poovey, *Planning a Christian Funeral* (Minneapolis: Augsburg, 1978), p. 21.
2. (Allen, Texas: Argus Communications, 1980), p. 107.
3. Elisabeth Kübler-Ross, *Death the Final Stage of Growth* (Englewood Cliffs, N.J.: Prentice-Hall, 1975), p. 26.
4. Bob Woodward, Scott Armstrong, *The Brethren: Inside the Supreme Court* (New York: Simon & Schuster, 1979), p. 157.

A VIOLENT DEATH

There are a number of elements that make difficult the funerals of those who die violently. One is the suddenness with which violent death almost always comes. At one moment a loved one is nearby, sharing a conversation; the next moment she is gone with no warning. Families stand numb, bewildered, unable to grasp or believe that death has happened. Unlike a terminal illness during which there is time for much anticipatory grieving, violent death comes like a thief in the night.

Often there is an element of absurdity, of "non-sense," which complicates the ever-present search for meaning that is part of most difficult deaths. A young woman whom I had confirmed was found dead in a bad area of a large city. No reason could be found for her death. It was the brutal act of a deranged individual. The young woman's family may never recover from their hurt.

Violent death may mutilate the body of the deceased to such a degree that the family may be denied the period of viewing with an open casket. Industrial and farm accidents, motor vehicle collisions, and trauma often leave the body in a condition that precludes viewing.

Deaths by homicide give rise to emotions which complicate the grieving process. The family feels a deep sense of anger toward the perpetrator of the act. There may be a desire for revenge. When the perpetrator is not known, a lengthy investigation may reopen a family's wounds each time they are consulted by the investigative authorities. Polly Doyle wrote in *Grief Counseling and Sudden Death* that a family may become "frozen at the level of imagining the violence with which their relative died. They find it difficult to deal with the death in terms of their own loss and sadness."[1] When the victim is a child, the powerlessness felt by the child's parents may cause them extreme anguish.

Anger often is directed at God. Such was the case with the friends of a young man who was killed while working on his car. The hoist suspending the automobile slipped and the boy was crushed. "Where," his friends asked, "was God when our friend needed him?"

Anger may even be directed at the victim, perhaps for getting into a situation in which he could lose his life. Since such anger is considered to be inappropriate, the guilt of the bereaved is increased. Family members who wish that they had died rather than the victim may experience survivor guilt. A father mourning the death of his son by a hunting accident said to me, "Why couldn't it have been me? I've lived my life."

To these emotions we bring the hope of the scripture. In the face of death's suddenness, Psalm 103 notes how transient our lives are, but the verse counters death's rude abruptness with the promise that the "steadfast love of the Lord is from everlasting to everlasting . . ." (103:17). The same note of transience is sounded by Jesus whose kingdom parable reminds us that "we know neither the day nor the hour of God's coming" (Matt. 25:13).

Paul's great statement of faith in Romans 8 recognizes that pain and suffering are endemic to a creation in travail (vss. 19-21) but it also holds firmly to the belief that the "sufferings of this present time are not worth comparing to the glory that is to be revealed to us" in God's kingdom (vs. 18).

In the face of the absurdity of violence, I Corinthians admits that we see "in a mirror dimly," but it promises that one day we will understand (13:12).

In Philippians Paul spoke of Jesus' violent death on the cross, but he also wrote of God's faithfulness in highly exalting Jesus and in giving him a "name" that has become the focus of worship for persons suffering persecution and violent death (2:5-11).

The sermon that follows sprang from the psalmist's cry of despair (22:1), which was echoed by Jesus on the Cross: "My God, my God, why hast thou forsaken me?" (Mark 15:34). I selected the text because of the number of bereaved family members who asked "Where was God when she needed him?"

A rabbi who was searching for God's presence in his wife's death wrote that "God was in the quiet gratitude of her joys. He was in the victory of her courage. He was also in her humor, which never forsook her."[2] Even in death, God may be found in unexpected places.

God is never far away. The psalmist's cry of despair becomes a cry of thanksgiving in the second half of the psalm (Ps. 22:22-31). Jesus went on to pray,

"Father, into thy hands I commit my spirit" (Luke 23:46).

Ultimately, how we live is more important than the manner of our dying. Elisabeth Kübler-Ross wrote that

> . . . dying is something that we human beings do continuously, not just at the end of our physical lives on this earth. The stages of dying . . . apply . . . to any significant change (e.g., retirement, moving to a new city, changing jobs, divorce) in a person's life, and change is a regular occurrence in human existence. If you can face and understand your ultimate death, perhaps you can learn to face and deal productively with each change that presents itself in your life. . . . And through a lifetime of such commitment, you can face your final end with peace and joy, knowing that you have lived your life well.[3]

The woman for whom this sermon was written lived such a life.

THE SERMON

Text: "My God, my God, why hast thou forsaken me?" *(Ps. 22:1; Mark 15:34b)*

There are events in life that seem to strain faith to its breaking point. That is my feeling about the events of this week. To hear of _____'s death and yet to believe that God loved her and loves us seems to stretch faith to the point where it no longer makes any sense. Some of you have said it: "If God loves and protects us, why was he not there for _____?"

God is light, the Bible says, but all we can see right now is the darkness of her death. God is love, the Bible tells us, but we've just lost someone who every day incarnated that love in the children she taught. Every fiber of our being cries out its protest to God: "Where were you when the drunken driver came careening down the highway, taking the life of one of the happiest and most loving persons we've ever known?" And I'm going to stand with you because _____ was my friend, and I share your hurt.

Annie Dillard wrote about listening to her pastor pray in church. He paused in the middle of the pastoral prayer and, giving vent to his frustration, said, "Lord, we bring you these petitions every week."[4] I can feel his frustration.

_____ was such a beautiful person. You know how hard it is on children when they move to a new community and a new school. Well, _____ was my son's first teacher when we moved here. She instinctively sensed his hurt, touched it, and helped him heal by the sheer warmth of her caring. She made parent-teacher conferences something to look forward to.

She and _____ (her husband) became active in the church. I always knew when she was in church. You could hear her laugh a mile away. She was my catalyst. While others sat quietly in the pews wondering whether or not it was all right to laugh in church, _____'s spontaneity allowed her laughter to break out. Once she would laugh at something I said, everyone else would join in.

She really knew how to pamper a preacher. I enjoy visiting in the homes of our families. The morning I went to visit _____, she was ready for me with coffee and banana cream pie—my favorite. I am going to miss her so much.

John Donne said that every person's death diminishes each of us. That is the way I feel. When _____ died, part of the warmth and laughter that she brought to me died as well. And if her death is that painful for me, how much more so for those of you who were closest to her? Where was God when _____ needed him?

We are not the first to ask the question. Elie Wiesel wrote of his experience in Auschwitz during the Second World War. All of the prisoners were made to witness the execution of two men and a boy. Out of the murmuring crowd came the question: "Where is God? Where is he?"[5]

The psalmist wrote "My God, my God, why hast thou forsaken me?" He told of those who mocked him, laughed at him in his pain.

Jesus hung upon the cross and in the despair of his dying asked the same question: "My God, my God, why . . . ?"

But in the concentration camp crowd behind Wiesel, another voice said, "He's there, hanging on that scaffold."

And one psalm later, the psalmist would remember that "The Lord is my shepherd . . ."

And on the cross, Jesus also remembered who had
given him life and continued to sustain it: "Father,
into thy hands I commit my spirit!" (Luke 23:46).

I don't know why _____ was killed in a
senseless accident. I don't know why such things
happen to anyone. But there are three certainties
that I would like to share with you.

I do know that we live in a society in which people
drink themselves into a drunken stupor and then go
out on the road and kill innocent people like
_____. That makes me angry.

I do know that there are two ways of channeling
this anger. I can turn it inward, focus on my hurt, and
let the bitterness fester like a wound, or I can
determine to do everything in my power at every
opportunity to get drunk drivers off the road.

And I know that when I hurt, as I do now, there is
only one thing that eases my pain: the belief that God
shares the hurt and, beyond the hurt, has given to
_____ a life in his presence that is free of the
sadness we feel.

Dorothee Soelle noted in her book *Suffering* that
faith has two essential elements. One of them is the
dark night of despair, the cross on which we are
hammered without being asked. The other element
is resurrection, the "unending affirmation of life that
arises in the dark night of the cross."[6] _____ has
experienced both of the elements. It remains for us
to try to continue to love as _____ did and as
God does, through every dark night of the cross and
into the light beyond.

Notes

1. (Springfield, Ill.: Charles C. Thomas, 1980), p. 105.
2. Jacob Philip Rudin, "Thoughts on My Wife's Death," in *But Not to Lose: A Book of Comfort for Those Bereaved*, ed. Austin H. Kutschner (New York: Frederick Fell, 1969), p. 42.
3. *Death the Final Stage of Growth* (Englewood Cliffs, N.J.: Prentice-Hall, 1975), p. 145.
4. *Holy the Firm* (New York: Harper, 1977), p. 58.
5. *Night*, foreword by Francois Mauriac; trans. Stella Rodway (New York: Avon Books, 1960), p. x.
6. Trans. Everett Kalin (Philadelphia: Fortress, 1975), p. 157.

SELECTED BIBLIOGRAPHY

A Service of Death and Resurrection, Supplemental Worship Resources 7. Nashville: Abingdon Press, 1979.

Bane, J. Donald; Kutscher, Austin H.; Neale, Robert E.; and Reeves, Robert B., Jr. *Death and Ministry.* New York: Seabury Press, 1975.

Becker, Ernest. *The Denial of Death.* New York: The Free Press, 1973.

Biddle, Perry H., Jr., *The Abingdon Funeral Manual.* Nashville: Abingdon, 1976; rev. 1984.

Blackwood, Andrew Watterson. *The Funeral.* Philadelphia: Westminster, 1941.

Bowers, Margaretta K.; Jackson, Edgar N., Knight, James A.; and LeShan, Lawrence. *Counseling the Dying.* San Francisco: Harper, 1964.

Bowman, Leroy. *The American Funeral.* Westport, Conn.: Greenwood Press, 1973.

Bunting, Ian. *Preaching at Funerals.* Grove booklets on Ministry and Worship. Bramcote Notts.

Buscaglia, Leo. *The Disabled and Their Parents.* New York: Holt, Rinehart, and Winston, 1983.

Cadenhead, Al, Jr. *The Minister's Manual for Funerals.* Nashville: Broadman, 1988.

Centering Corporation (P.O. Box 3367) Omaha, NE. *Miscarriage; Newborn Death; No New Baby; Why Mine?*

Chakour, Charles M. *Brief Funeral Meditations.* Nashville: Abingdon, 1971.

De Frain, John; Ernst, Linda; Taylor, Jacque. *Coping With Sudden Infant Death.* Toronto: Lexington Books, 1982.

Dodd, Robert V. *When Someone You Love Dies: An Exploration of Death for Children.* Nashville: Abingdon, 1989.

————. *When They All Go Home: What to Do After the Funeral.* Nashville: Abingdon, 1989.

Doyle, Polly. *Grief Counseling and Sudden Death.* Springfield, Ill.: Charles C. Thomas, 1980.

Dunkle, William F., Jr. and Joseph D. Quillian, Jr. *Companion to the Book of Worship.* Nashville: Abingdon, 1970.

Enright, D. J., ed. *Oxford Book of Death.* New York: Oxford Press, 1983.

Franklyn, Mary Beth. *After Pregnancy Loss.* Nashville: Discipleship Resources, 1988.

Fulton, Robert, Ed. *Death and Iniquity.* New York: John Wiley and Sons, 1965.

Gerkin, Charles V. *Crisis Experience in Modern Life.* Nashville: Abingdon, 1979.

Green, Morris; Osterweis, Marian; Solomon, Frederic, eds. *Bereavement: Reactions, Consequences, and Care.* Washington, D.C.: National Academy Press, 1984.

Griffin, Mary; Felsenthal, Carol. *A Cry for Help.* Garden City, N.Y.: Doubleday and Co., 1983.

Hewett, John H. *After Suicide.* Philadelphia: Westminster, 1980.

Hughes, Robert. *A Trumpet in Darkness: Preaching to Mourners.* Philadelphia: Fortress, 1985.

Irion, Paul E. *The Funeral and the Mourners.* New York: Abingdon, 1954.

————. *The Funeral: Vestige or Value?* Nashville: Abingdon, 1966.

Jackson, Edgar N. *The Christian Funeral.* New York: Channel Press, 1966.

———. *For the Living.* Des Moines, Iowa: Channel Press, 1963.

———. *When Someone Dies.* Philadelphia: Fortress, 1971.

Jewett, John H. *After Suicide.* Philadelphia: Westminster, 1980.

Johnson, Sherry E. *After a Child Dies: Counseling Bereaved Families.* New York: Springer, 1987.

Kelsey, Morton T. *Afterlife: The Other Side of Dying.* New York: Crossroad, 1988.

Kübler-Ross, Elisabeth. *Death the Final Stage of Growth.* Englewood Cliffs, N.J.: Prentice-Hall, 1975.

———. *On Death and Dying.* New York: Macmillan, 1969.

Kutscher, Austin H., ed. *But Not to Lose: A Book of Comfort for Those Bereaved.* New York: Frederick Fell, 1969.

Lifton, Robert Jay. *The Broken Connection.* New York: Basic Books, 1979.

Marty, Martin. *Friendship.* Allen, Texas: Argus Communications, 1980.

Mills, Liston O., ed. *Perspectives on Death.* Nashville: Abingdon, 1969.

Mitford, Jessica. *The American Way of Death.* New York: Simon & Schuster, 1963.

Moltmann, Jürgen. *The Crucified God.* Trans. Wilson, R. A.; and Bowden, John. New York: Harper & Row, 1974.

Neale, Robert E. *The Art of Dying.* New York: Harper & Row, 1973.

Nouwen, Henri J. M. *A Letter of Consolation.* San Francisco: Harper & Row, 1982.

———. *In Memoriam.* Notre Dame, Ind.: Ave Maria Press, 1980.

———. *The Wounded Healer.* New York: Doubleday Image Books, 1979.

Oates, Wayne. *Pastoral Care and Counseling in Grief and Separation.* Philadelphia: Fortress, 1976.

Poovey, W. A. *Planning a Christian Funeral.* Minneapolis: Augsburg, 1978.

Raphael, Beverly. *The Anatomy of Bereavement.* New York: Basic Books, 1983.

Rest, Friedrich. *Funeral Handbook.* Valley Forge, Penn.: Judson Press, 1985.

Rubin, Theodore Isaac. *The Angry Book.* New York: Colliers Books, 1969.

Schiff, Harriet Sarnoff. *The Bereaved Parent.* New York: Crown, 1977.

Schneidman, Edwin. *Definition of Suicide.* New York: John Wiley and Sons, 1985.

Schoenberg, Bernard, et al. *Anticipatory Grief.* New York: Columbia University Press, 1974.

Schoenberg, B. Mark. *Bereavement Counseling.* Westport, Conn.: Greenwood, 1980.

Schwiebert, Pat and Kirk, Paul. *Still to Be Born.* Perinatal Loss; 2116 N.E. 18th Ave.; Portland, Oregon.

Soulen, Richard N., ed. *Care for the Dying.* Atlanta: John Knox, 1975.

Stone, Howard W. *Crisis Counseling.* Philadelphia: Fortress, 1976.

Switzer, David K. *The Dynamics of Grief: Its Source, Pain, and Healing.* Nashville: Abingdon, 1970.

―――. *The Minister as Crisis Counselor.* Nashville: Abingdon, 1974.

Swords, Liam, ed. *Funeral Homilies.* Mahwah, N.J. : Paulist Press, 1985.

Taking Time, National Institutes of Health; National Cancer Institute; Bethesda, Maryland, 1986.

Thielicke, Helmut. *Living with Death.* Trans. Geoffrey W. Bromiley. Grand Rapids, Mich.: Eerdmans, 1983.

Thompson, Charlotte E. *Raising a Handicapped Child.* New York: Ballantine, 1987.

Weems, Lovett H., Jr. *Christian Funeral: A Guide.* Nashville: Abingdon, 1986.

Westberg, Granger. *Good Grief.* Philadelphia: Fortress, 1962.

Willimon, William H. *Worship as Pastoral Care.* Nashville: Abingdon, 1979.

Yalom, Irvin D. *Existential Psychotherapy.* New York: Basic Books, 1980.